James Haynes

History of the Methodist Episcopal Church

in Omaha and suburbs

James Haynes

History of the Methodist Episcopal Church
in Omaha and suburbs

ISBN/EAN: 9783337262488

Printed in Europe, USA, Canada, Australia, Japan

Cover: Foto ©Lupo / pixelio.de

More available books at **www.hansebooks.com**

Yours etc.,
James Haynes.

HISTORY

OF THE

METHODIST EPISCOPAL CHURCH

IN

OMAHA AND SUBURBS.

BY

REV. JAMES HAYNES.

WITH AN INTRODUCTION BY

BISHOP JOHN P. NEWMAN, D.D.

PRINTED FOR THE AUTHOR
BY THE OMAHA PRINTING COMPANY.
1895.

CONTENTS

CHAPTER I

INITIAL WORDS.

CHAPTER II

PROGRESS OF THE CHURCH

CHAPTER III.

PRELIMINARY REMARKS.

A few living citizens remember when Omaha began being built—Omaha soon known abroad—The wide-awake itinerant soon on the ground—The first sermon ever preached in Omaha was by Peter Cooper, in 1854—A claim made that Wm. Simpson, of Iowa, had preached at an earlier date is probably erroneous.

HISTORY.

The earliest acts and achievements of the Church acquired from the oldest citizens—Isaac F. Collins the first pastor in Omaha—The site of the first Methodist house of worship—The lots donated—Description of the building—Dedicated December, 1856—The first Quarterly meeting held Sept. 12th, 1856, Wm. H Goode, presiding—Names of communicants—The fourth session of the Kansas-Nebraska Annual conference was held at Omaha, Bishop Scott, presiding—Quarterly meeting held at the present corner of Twenty-fifth street and Ames avenue, where a class had been organized—John M Chivington succeeds Mr. Collins to the pastorate in Omaha, in 1857—The regular succession of pastors follows, including sketches of each to the date of publication.................page 36

CHAPTER IV.

CHURCH BUILDING IN SUBURBS

The need of suburban churches accounted for—The first movement towards forming a second Society—Holding Sunday-school in a rented store building on Twenty-third street between Izard and Nicholas—The mission prospered—A house was soon built at Izard and Twenty-first, a pastor invited, and a regular organization effected—Names of Trus-

CHAPTER V.

THE SUNDAY SCHOOL.

CHAPTER VI.

HANSCOM PARK CHURCH.

CHAPTER VII.

TRINITY CHURCH.

CHAPTER VIII.

SOUTH OMAHA CHURCH.

This Society regarded as suburban—T. B. Hilton assigned as pastor, September, 1886—No class yet organized—He accomplishes the building of a church and parsonage—L. H. Eddleblute becomes pastor in 1887—Cutting down a high bank requires a new house of worship—Church Extension Society helps—In 1889 D. Marquette is appointed pastor—The new house cost $4,000—Was dedicated—The number of members exceed one hundred—C. N. Dawson takes charge, September, 1890—The church is burned January 18th, 1893—Public sympathy aroused—Another, and the third, house built on the same site—Dedicated January 21st, 1894—Present membership more than three hundred—Mr. Dawson serving the fifth year..............page 165

SKETCHES OF MINISTERS.

List of Illustrations.

LIST OF ILLUSTRATIONS.

DEDICATION.

To my Wife and Sons, who have taken so much interest in my labors and success in the preparation of this book, I affectionately dedicate the volume.

JAMES HAYNES.

PREFACE.

The reader who takes interest in the perusal of this volume will learn that its production cost no small measure of industry to compile, arrange and write the matter filling its pages after the lapse of forty years since the introduction of Methodism in Omaha. Old records, minutes of business meetings and memoranda containing the transactions of the Churches must be consulted in preparing for preservation a continuous narrative of occurrences.

To group events long since forgotten by most of the surviving actors, and to make mention of persons, incidents, and objects once familiar to the living, is part of the work of the Church historian. These things must be sought from sources the most reliable, whether recorded or unwritten, often at a perplexing disadvantage; and the first to gather the facts from which the narrative is constructed is often confronted with obstacles not easy to overcome.

Not many years since and at different times newspaper reporters attempted writing of the early history of the Church first attracting the attention of the people of this city; but these hurried scribes usually took notes from the lips of the oldest settlers whose recollection is not always to be depended upon; hence, there is not an agreement in statements, names and dates. To authenticate this history is part of the purpose of this writing. There are, however, many incidents in the annals of every long-established Church that must be treated, if used at all, after getting the most trustworthy information within reach, without an appeal to records.

Except dates and other guides to the earliest happenings are accessible, the author sets up no claim to inerrancy in the recital of the story of the progress of the local Churches. Yet, in the main, it will be found accurate in statement and faithful in theory. The intention has been little more than to gather matter and collate history, which, if not done now, may be almost wholly lost to the denomination.

Assistance must be acknowledged from Revs. H. T. Davis, Dr. J. B. Maxfield, C. N. Dawson, T. C. Clendening and John Dale, as well as Mrs. Hawver and Messrs. Sorenson, Hawver, Marston, Burns, McLain, Ball, Rose brothers, Young, Toms, Bexton and Ryerson.

In the compiling and note making the writer has taken real pleasure, as well as in the preparation of the book for the press; and hopes it may furnish no small mede of satisfaction to the reader, as it presents reminiscences that will, without doubt, be gratifying to the survivors of the membership of long ago, as well as history for the younger men who may be searching for statistics and ecclesiastical data of times agone.

THE AUTHOR.

Omaha, July 15th, 1895.

INTRODUCTION.

The Church historian has a higher mission than the writer of profane history. It is for him to record the origin of Churches, however small their beginning, and however fierce the struggle to maintain their existence. In such a record are the elements of romance often more fascinating than the dream of the poet, and of heroism more worthy of bronze and marble than achievements upon the field of carnage. These Christian heroes often work out of sight; rarely are they seen or known beyond the limited circle of a handful of ardent associates, and seldom cheered by the blast of trumpet or the sound of drum; but they are moved by a sublime faith in the power of Christianity to renovate society, to correct social evils, to transform the heart and life of man and make earth a heaven; they build churches, support public worship, and that out of an income by no means large.

The history of a Church is the history of a community: with it are forever associated the memories of marriage, of baptism and of burial, three significant events in our human life. Within the holy influence of the sanctuary manhood is formed, womanhood is developed and citizenship is ennobled. As a rule the Church represents the intelligence, the wealth and the morality of the city, and thereby becomes the bond of social union and the safeguard of public prosperity. Not unfrequently, the sacred edifice remains for many years the landmark to indicate the growth of the town from a small beginning to one of metropolitan proportions; and old men point to it with pride, as when in times past it stood alone, but is now surrounded with houses of merchandise and banks of wealth.

All this is more emphatically true of Methodism than of

any other branch of the Christian Church. The Methodist is a pioneer; he is among the first on the ground; he is the builder of cities, the founder of schools, and the organizer of public charities. Methodism is a living force embracing all the personal, domestic, social, national, political and commercial interests of the people. Its history has been one of moral revolution and the elevation of public sentiment wherever its representatives have been permitted to develop their self-sustaining and self-expanding power. The whole of the Mighty West is a monument of the piety, zeal and courage of the Methodist itinerant, who leads the van of our civilization, and stands on the mountain top of vision and beholds the dawn of the coming of a brighter day. Other demonstrations follow in this luminous wake, but they come to occupy fields already prepared by those who had faith and bravery to anticipate the wants and opportunities of the future. How true is this of Omaha Methodism, whose history is coincident with the marvelous growth and expansion of our proud midland city, the gateway to the great Pacific.

The present work illustrates the story of the Methodist Church in the city of Omaha; and no one is more competent to delineate its features than the author, as he is a writer of our best English, clear, direct and graphic. His communications to our Church papers are readily accepted and read with interest. Born in Brooke county, Virginia, in 1826, he came to the West in his youth and began acquiring a classical education at a Seminary in Mount Pleasant, Iowa, and pursued his later studies in our Wesleyan University in the same city. The great state of Iowa was the theater of his ministry, where he was pastor and presiding elder till his superannuation, and, in the latter effective capacity, sat in the cabinet with some of our greatest Bishops. He has known Bishops Morris, Simpson, Janes, Ames, Scott, Baker, Thompson, Wiley, Kingsley, and all those now occupying our Episcopal bench.

Since 1875 he has been a resident of Omaha, and for twenty years has been familiar with the growth of Methodism therein. He has seen our Church here advance from a small beginning to its present splendid condition. When he came to this city, Omaha had not a paved street, and but 20,000 inhabitants, but now he looks out upon its noble thoroughfares and its teeming population of more than 140,000 enterprising, intelligent, and hopeful citizens. Such a man is a competent historian and his work will be read with absorbing interest.

JOHN P. NEWMAN,
Resident Bishop.

OMAHA, January 1st, 1895.

METHODISM IN OMAHA.

CHAPTER I.

INITIAL WORDS.

THE story of a local Church is usually construed as commonplace; which notion mostly grows out of our being on the ground where the incidents transpired. But this exception should detract nought from the interest in reading, if the matters rehearsed are worth preserving. More or less remote dates, and the names of participants whose deeds and words made the history of the Church of earlier times, would, it seems, the more likely invite an investigation.

The marked features of this volume are in its having been made up of things—instances and incidents—both old and new. The composition is a recital of matters of fact, presenting outlines of living and actual history, abstracted in a measure from the written records of the Churches. It treats almost solely of things concerning the earlier and continuous work by the preachers and people of Methodism in Omaha and suburbs, first in introducing and next in perpetuating the Church of their choice west of the Missouri river.

The very beginning of efforts was successful, though without the facilities of the present, in laying a foundation firm enough to withstand the contending and spirited opposition that followed. The first decade of its existence was marked by conflicts that might have sundered the organization but for the loyalty of its adherents to God and His cause, and their fidelity to the government in which they had citizenship. But early in the next ten years the little Society was called upon to experience vicissitudes of another kind. The changing condition of the thrifty and pretentious city made an impression on the Church that it should seize the opportunity to improve its financial strength. After deliberation a course was defined, and, nearly at once, their property was converted to another use, and money was borrowed to procure a new and better site and house of worship. This new venture, however, resulted in the loss of all the property owned by the Society in the commencement of the third decade.

The undaunted household now having reached its majority, profiting by past experience, bravely began providing another place of worship, and from that day henceforth has been prospered. The monument now adorning the corner of Twentieth and Davenport streets is an index of their achievements.

When Isaac F. Collins, in 1855, opened the Bible and began his ministry in Omaha, and Wil-

liam H. Goode, his presiding elder, held the first
Quarterly conference in the aspiring village,
neither, perhaps, could forecast such an outcome
from such an insignificant beginning as has been
bequeathed their followers. But they laid the
foundation that has been built upon, enlarged, and
enjoyed by their successors till the communicants
and friends of the denomination now number a
multitude. The edifices that have been reared to
make sittings for the accumulating throng dot the
town as light houses betokening the foresight and
energy of the citizens who have contributed
towards their erection, and as indices of the moral
and religious life of the several communities in
which they are located.

The original Church worked alone till 1870,
and had been served in the pastoral office by men
of sterling worth and ability, namely, Davis,
Lemon, Slaughter. Westwood and De La Matyr.
Since the organization of other charges, the old
Church has been ministered to by such as Messrs.
Gue. Wright, Britt, Fisher, Maxfield, Stewart,
Savidge, McKaig, House, Merrill and Crane, from
one to three years each, in the order in which their
names occur. Some of these latter, all of whom
are yet living, were learned in theology, and without mitre or gown preached Jesus, and "the common people heard them gladly." The memorable
years of 1876 and 1877, including the administra-
tions of Leroy F. Britt and Dr. Hugh D. Fisher, .

the loss of the property of the First Church was threatened, and then culminated in the surrender of every dollar's worth to eastern bondholders. But Dr. Fisher's energy, by the aid of the Trustees and others, speedily brought about the rearing of a wooden church on Davenport street in which his people worshiped, and for several years succeeding was occupied by the Society.

The year 1869 is in the memory of not a few old settlers as the period in which a beginning was made which resulted a little later in the organization of a class in the northern part of the city. A Sunday-school was first begun, by the aid of the members of the First Church, attracting the attention of the neighborhood. Soon afterwards Moses F. Shinn several times dispensed the gospel in the shade of large trees which stood at that date near the present corner of Twenty-fourth and Cuming streets. This movement not long after was followed by an effort to build a house for the use of the Society and Sunday-school. In this the mother Church assisted liberally both in providing money and members. And a little later a contract was let to Rose brothers to erect a good, two-story frame building, which at this time stands on the east side of Eighteenth street south of California, and is owned and occupied by the Swedish Methodist as a place of worship. The former site, and where the Second church was built, was at the corner of Twenty-first and Izard streets; but it was moved from this spot in 1874 to its present location. and was known for several years as the Eighteenth Street Methodist Church.

On the completion of the building, as it was once seen on Izard street, it was immediately made use of: a pastor was appointed, and, henceforward, it was operated independently. There was no opposition in that part of the city, and the growth of population soon made it an important factor in religious work, by furnishing sittings for the church-goers in contiguous neighborhoods. The location was central to the population, and it was an error in the judgment of those who permitted or controlled its removal to another part of town.

The Society which at first constituted the new organization was served in the pastorate successively by Geo. W. De La Matyr in 1870: Cyrus A. King in 1871; C. McKelvey in 1872, and Joseph H. Presson. 1873—a long year, the time of the meeting of the Conference having been changed from spring to fall.* But to the Society's detriment has twice removed: first to the place above named, and. lastly, to Seward street, which it at present maintains. While worshiping on Eighteenth street it was served in the pulpit by men of experience such as T. B. Lemon, I. N. Pardee, P. C. Johnson, W. K Beans, J. W. Shank and J. B. Leedom. Under the administration of Mr. Pardee a comfortable two-story frame parsonage was built on the north side of the church. which afterwards

made a pleasant home for the pastors.   It yet stands
on the same site.

Several influential persons united with the
Society at this place, and, for a time, substantial
prosperity encouraged the membership.   Later
in its history, and about 1882, some discourage-
ments were met with, assuring its friends that its
mission in that location had been fulfilled.   Still
later the number of attendants diminished, a few
unpleasant occurrences ensued, settling at once the
uselessness of the Society's attempting longer to
continue services in that place.

In the summer of 1883 the conclusion was
reached that a new location must be sought.   The
property was disposed of by sale, and a lot at the
north-east corner of Twenty-second and Seward
streets was acquired by purchase.   Soon afterwards, R. L. Marsh having been appointed pastor,
a canvassing for subscriptions was begun.   With
untiring activity the soliciting was kept up by visiting citizens in the vicinity, and business men,
generally.   The pastor's success was such that. in
the autumn of 1884, the corner stone of a new edifice
was laid, and the progress made in its erection
allowed of its being dedicated in the spring of 1885
to the worship of God.

The following September C. W. Savidge became
the pastor of the new Society and popularly served
for three years.   He was succeeded by W. M.
Worley, one year; and H. A. Crane, three years.

when the latter accepted an appointment as missionary to Bombay, India, where he still remains. Dr. D. K. Tindall was his successor in 1892, and, remaining two years, left the charge prospering, but was removed to man the Grand Island district. W. K. Beans, having served Trinity Church in this city five years, was transferred to this Church, October, 1894.

About the first of July, 1895, Rev. W. K. Beans was transferred to the First Methodist Church, Salt Lake, and was given also the office of presiding elder of Ogden district, Utah. Rev. H. A. Barton, of Madison, Nebraska, has since been appointed his successor at Seward Street.

This Society is now composed of intelligent and thrifty people, who are carrying on aggressively all lines of Church work, and their prospects are such as to call out their best efforts. But its location is not the most desirable, nor the best for convenience of access, respecting which if the site were on a line of street railway the Church would be the means of inducing more people doubtless to attend its week-time and Sabbath services. The Society, nevertheless, in spite of this drawback, is a great power for good in making moral impressions on the residents of that vicinity, though it may come short of accomplishing all that is intended in the locating and establishing a house of worship.

CHAPTER II.

THE FIRST CHURCH.

ASIDE from the clergy, an ecclesiastical organization of the First Methodist Episcopal Church has been maintained in Omaha, without intermission, since its beginning in 1855. The new village at that date began improving rapidly, till at the close of 1856 the population was estimated at 1,600. Among the newcomers of that year were some Methodists, who, finding already a church building had been projected and a brick edifice begun, attached themselves to the Society and gave aid to the enterprise. Before the ending of 1856 these pioneers enjoyed the occupancy of the coveted place of worship and witnessed its dedication.

But a financial panic in the summer of 1857 for a time held in check the progress of both the village and the Society. The depression continued through the year 1858, and the Church had a struggle for maintenance. The pastor subsisted on a meager allowance, and there was a general curtailment of current expenses. A measure of relief was experienced the next year when gold was discovered in Colorado. Omaha felt the impulse, as this was an outfitting point: and merchants prepared themselves with goods and wares such as gold seekers needed, and a lively market was the result.

Soon afterwards, however, and while prosperity was cheering the city and Church, the disturbance incident to the breaking out of the Rebellion began making an impression on public opinion that was not helpful to the little flock of enthusiastic Methodists. As in nearly every place in the North, the local Church was not a comfortable home for any whose sympathies were not in behalf of the Federal government. Patriots were outspoken to the extent of frequently making themselves offensive to others, and the Church did not succeed as if there had been no want of fellowship. Before the surrender at Appomattox, nevertheless, there was an uplift given the efforts of the brethren who had been bearing the burden of the Church. The membership in 1864 was only eighty and a few probationers; but good salaries were paid for ministerial services, indicating that material prosperity had enabled the few to contribute in larger sums to pastoral support. Henceforth the Church began with energy to put forth efforts to accomplish its purposes.

The continual coming of people soon increased the population of the city to 4,000, though additions to the Church membership were few compared with the popular increase. Effective revivals seem to have been rare and of little avail in making greater the number of communicants. This may be explained, perhaps, by taking into account the coarse quality of many who sought homes and employment in the new-made city. The building of the Union Pacific railway now in progress attracted a large number of young men without families who cared for nought but a living and sport. All manner of doubtful and immoral practices, ruinous to virtue and the souls of the participants, were common as the mud in the streets. The Church withstood all of the opposition growing out of these things, though tried as by fire. and preserved, as an organization, its identity and respect.

The original church on Thirteenth street had been in use as a place of worship about eleven years when a controlling number of the Trustees thought the property too valuable to be used longer for religious services. The Society at this date, 1867, having acquired friends and accumulated moneyed ability was encouraged as much as to begin speculating whether the building and site might not be disposed of for a sum that would largely aid in the erection of a new and better-planned house. Others of the Board suggested the making of such changes in the structure as to provide a second-story auditorium, and partition the first floor for mercantile purposes. Neither of these parties prevailed, as the sequel will show.

At a little later period, however, there was an

agreement to sell the property. It was advertised, but, failing to induce a ready bidder, was soon withdrawn from the market. The next movement that met with favor was to transform the building and rent it; and almost at once the work was begun. An addition was made to the south side of fifteen feet and to the north side of twenty-two feet, both the full length of the house, fifty-eight feet. These additions were two stories in height, and the story of the church being high, in adjusting the roof and putting joist the right height from the lower floor, a second story was secured for the entire area. Iron columns were erected and beams were placed across the front of the newly modeled structure, giving it the appearance of a business block. The first floor was converted into stores and the second was partitioned for twelve office rooms, at an expense of $11,575. There was an immediate demand for such rooms, and by the 8th of December, 1867. they were all rented, bringing revenue to the Trustees amounting to the sum of $6,280 the first year.

The money accruing from this source was used to liquidate the cost of the improvements, as the following excerpt from the minutes of the Trustees will distinctly explain:

"RESOLVED, That we place the Thirteenth-street property in the hands of G. W. Homan, N. P. Isaacs and G. W. Forbes to be by them leased, and the moneys retained for the purpose of meeting the cost of the improvements now being made And the said Homan, Isaacs and Forbes shall have possession

of said premises, and be entitled to said moneys till all liabili-
ties they incur in effecting said improvements shall be provided
for by current income from rent or any other source "

The date of the passage of this resolution is
September 5th, 1867; and the progress of debt can-
celing may be ascertained from the minutes of a
meeting of March 3d, 1868, when the secretary
was authorized to burn six promissory notes aggre-
gating $6,376.94.

The Society was now churchless, and had to
make such provision as possible for a room in which
to worship. The Trustees effected a contract with
the German Methodists, whose church was located
on the north side of Davenport, between Four-
teenth and Fifteenth streets, to be allowed to use
their house for preaching services, the considera-
tion for which privilege was the tender of the pulpit and seats taken from the house that was being
re-constructed. Also an offer was made for the
purpose of acquiring greater accommodation at the
German church, the trustees agreeing to pay $15.00
a month, half the janitor's fee and one-half of the
expense of heating and lighting the house, for the
use of a class-room. The aforesaid church building was a wooden structure with a basement which
was divided into rooms suitable for the holding of
class meetings, which, with the last named bargain
remaining in force, might be used after the Society
had changed its more public services to another
place. Such change was in contemplation. Rev.

H. C. Westwood at this juncture having succeeded to the pastorate of the charge insisted that a more pretentious and inviting place be provided in which he might preach. The Academy of Music was hired at $25.00 per Sunday, and the congregation met for a time in the most ornamental room in the city. These arrangements were made that the people might have a place of meeting during the interim after vacating the old church and the construction of a new house.

Almost at once the Trustees began planning for the rearing of a new and more commodious temple. The beginning was made by procuring two lots of G. W. Forbes at the south-east corner of Seventeenth street and Capitol avenue, fronting on the latter, as a location for both a church and parsonage. Bishop Ames had interested himself in the development of Methodism in Omaha, and the Trustees advised with him respecting a mode of procedure. On August 5th, 1867, the secretary of the Board was instructed to address him on the subject of effecting a loan. Probably the Bishop had counseled to this purpose; and *how* to effect the getting of a loan appears now to be the point the Trustees wished to settle.

An agreement was reached that nothing would be done at building till the next spring; and there was employed as much of the skill of their best accountants as to determine the extent of the indebtedness of the Society for which some of the

Trustees were held. At a meeting on March 3d, 1868, the object was stated to be the ascertaining the amount of indebtedness, and to provide a way to concentrate it in one permanent loan. The Treasurer reported that the Omaha National Bank held notes to the amount of $7,185 signed by three or more of the Trustees; and that the First National had $2,200 in notes endorsed by the same persons: besides a note held by Wm. Dorson of $2,000, and an overdraft from one of the banks of $190. At this same meeting Geo. W. Forbes was made a committee to negotiate a loan in New York, at a low rate of interest, to the amount of not more than $20,000.

Under date of April 28th, 1868, the following proceedings are recorded :

"On motion, the Board resolved to build a parsonage costing not more than $1,400, and brothers Forbes and Homan were appointed a building committee. On motion, brother J. W. Tousley was appointed to solicit subscriptions for the purpose of building a parsonage.

SAMUEL HAWVER,
Secretary."

At a meeting of the Trustees, May 11th, 1868, Rev. H. C. Westwood was added to the committee to secure a loan for the purpose of building a new church.

Pastor Westwood took part in the writing and issuing of coupon bonds, sixty in number, of the denomination of $500.00 each to run ten years at ten per cent. per annum, secured by both the old and the new property. The better times, as construed by the Trustees, warranted the hazarding of all their property, now considered very valuable for the purpose of providing a place of worship. Brother Westwood was despatched to New York to effect the sale of the bonds; but meeting with difficulty not anticipated, he wrote for instructions. And at a meeting of the Board, November 3d, 1868, a communication was read from him asking if he should dispose of the bonds below par. In answer the following resolution was ordered to be forwarded to him by the Secretary:

"RESOLVED, That, after consulting Bishop Ames, Bro. Isaacs, and as many as feel an interest and are competent to give good advice, you are hereby authorized to act on your own best judgment in regard to selling the bonds at less than par."

Mr. Westwood returned from the East and was present at a meeting of the Trustees, November 30th, at which he stated that he arrived in New York in a fearful money crisis, and had failed to make sale of but few of the bonds. The bonds were in the market, and afterwards all but one were disposed of.

A contract was let for stone with which to build the basement of the new church at $7.50 per mason's perch of twenty-four feet. A building committee was appointed consisting of G. W. Forbes, G. W. Homan, G. W. Frost, Samuel Hawver and J. W. Tousley, at the date of July 24th, 1868.

Matters seem to be adjusting themselves favorable to having a new house, after an interim of too great duration to promote the best interests of the Church. The anxiety of the brethren had been put to a severe tension, but there was now a relaxing of their solicitude, and, in its stead, hopefulness.

The following-named persons were Trustees at this date, namely, G. W. Forbes, G. W. Homan, J. G. Behm, N. P. Isaacs, J. R. Steel, J. W. Tousley, John Ritchie, Samuel Hawver and J. J. McLain—9, a full board. Their arrangements were now perfected, and the money on hand for prosecuting the work of building a house of their own for occupation. Already a new parsonage had been begun, and was made ready for use in the time of Mr. Westwood's pastorate, in the autumn or winter of 1868. The site was on the north-east corner of the lots owned by the Society. This building afforded comfortable quarters for the preachers, and continued to be used as a parsonage till surrendered, with the other property of the Church, to the bondholders, in 1876; and was razed a year afterwards to make room for Hitchcock's brick row, the latter having been torn down by Federal authority, June, 1894.

The greater and much more expensive project of erecting a sanctuary was under way. The contract for the carpenter work had been let to Mr. Barringer, the brick work to John Withnell, and the painting to Messrs. Marston & Clark. The beginning was made in 1868, and the house was dedicated March 21st, 1869, both during the pastorate of Rev. H. C. Westwood. Mr. Westwood left the charge in July following, and Moses F.

SEVENTEENTH STREET CHURCH.

Shinn supplied the pulpit for several weeks till the arrival of Rev. Gilbert De La Matyr, who at once assumed the administration under more favorable circumstances. His having a good auditorium and restful sittings, the place was attractive; and his superior gifts in the pulpit added very much to the popularity of this place of worship.

The dimensions of the building were thirty-two feet in width by seventy feet in length, with a sub-basement, and an audience room on the third floor. But the house as it appeared for the last quarter of a century was only a chapel, and but the beginning of that which was originally contemplated. The great arch sprung on the north side was contrived to admit of all the brick below the circle being removed, that an opening large enough for all purposes might be made when the main structure should be reared. But the putting up of the main edifice was never attempted. The Society had even ventured beyond its financial ability in that which had already been done in building.

The sub-basement was divided into rooms and plastered, and a furnace set for warming the stories above. The basement floor, after leaving ample room in the lobby at the main entrance on the west for ingress and egress, and for reaching the two stairways conducting to the auditorium, was partitioned to make a lecture room and class-rooms. The audience room occupied almost the whole area of the third floor, and was seated with cherry pews having slat bottoms. The furniture of the pulpit —desk, table and chairs—was neat and becoming to the house of God. A small gallery was foisted at the front end above the exit to the stairs which accommodated the choir or a Sunday-school class. The seating capacity was about four hundred and seventy-five; and the edifice cost, including the furnishing, not much less than $20,000. In the rear of the church, on a strong frame, the bell was hung that was purchased for the old church in 1857, and had been preserved since dispensing with its use on Thirteenth street.

The architectural design of the building was Gothic, with heavy buttresses on the four corners and on the outer corners of the tower which projected frontward from the west wall. The buttresses were not carried above the roof and were surmounted by sharp wooden pinnacles. The tower was pierced with an opening for a large entrance door to the basement, and for a great ornamental window lighting the front end of the auditorium.

This structure was torn down in May of 1894 even to the upturning and removal from the premises of the rough and cut stone of which the walls of the sub-basement were constructed, and can henceforth remain only in the recollection of those who often worshiped in its sanctum and others who may have frequently glanced at its perspective. The struggle of those who were

directly concerned in the accomplishment of its
erection might be told by N. P. Isaacs and G. W.
Homan, if living; and Hawver, Steel, Tousley,
Burns, Forbes, McLain and Ritchie, who are yet
alive, can recite the sacrifices required to manage
the business and pay for the completion of the
house so lately demolished by the United States
government. Many members very little less interested, and attendants upon the services, as well as
faithful workers in the Sunday-school, though
taking no positive part in the business management of affairs, namely, M. G. McKoon, C. L.
Garrison, W. G. Pigman, T. J. Staley. Horace
Newman, L. R. Whitmore, R. D. Hills, Cyrus
Rose, J. W. Arnold, P. T. Downs, E. A. Parmelee, Albert Rose, A. M. Clark, J. M. Marston and
others, might disclose incidents that would invest
this chapter with lively interest. The gospel was
dispensed from its pulpit during the nine years it
was used by our people by some men eminent in
the ministry, including several bishops; and many
an impressive service was held in the lecture room
as might be certified by numerous witnesses who
attended and took part in the meetings led in turns
by Frost, Tousley, Roberts and Lange. It was
regarded for several years as a hallowed place,
and was the mid-week resort of the most ardent
communicants.

Scarcely any less than the pastors the ruling
officers of the Church have been conspicuous in

promoting its general weal. Whoever may read the story of the earlier history of the Society in this city will find associated with it the names before mentioned, and, in addition, those of P. A. Demorest, Edwin Loveland, Geo. C. Ritchie, J. G. Behm and Alfred Burley, as intimately connected with all that was accomplished and actively concerned in directing the business.

The church was vacated July 8th, 1877, and the Society was again left without a place of worship of its own, and the Masonic Hall on the north-west corner of Sixteenth and Capitol avenue was hired and used till a new building was put up. But excluding us from the Seventeenth street place of worship was the most serious mishap that ever overtook this already venerable organization, not alone because of the loss of all of its property, but the impairing of the credit of the Church was much in the way of future efforts. The rallying of forces who comprehended the situation, however, brought to pass that which was seemingly not possible. The energetic and tireless worker and expert organizer, Dr. H. D. Fisher, serving now the second year of his pastorate, summoned to his aid the best business talent of the Church, and at a session of the Quarterly conference, April 3d, 1877, at his instance, the board of Trustees was reconstructed. He nominated some new ones, and the roster was made to read, C. C. Housel, President: T. J. Staley, Secretary; M. G. McKoon, S. T. Josselyn, J. L.

Webster, E. L. Stone, Sam'l Hawver, J. J. McLain
and A. M. Clark, all of whom, at this writing, still
survive.

The membership at this date numbered 232,
but a discouraging proportion of them was little
able to make subscriptions of such sums as were
adequate to the necessities of the occasion. The
Society was diligently canvassed, but the sum
needing was short to the extent that a loan of
$3,000 was sought and obtained of the Church
Extension Society, of Philadelphia, at six per cent.
per annum, which enabled the Trustees to begin
devising business plans preparatory to the construction of the third house of worship since the
first sermon was preached by a Methodist in Omaha.

Preliminary to this attempt a lot was purchased
sixty-six feet west of Seventeenth street on the
south side of Davenport as a site, at an expenditure of $1,800. The plans of a building now had
to be decided upon for the joint purposes of a
church and parsonage. Before much time had
elapsed C. F. Driscol, an architect, produced plans,
including suggestions made by the pastor and Trustees, which were adopted. The parties authorized contracted for brick for the foundation and
chimneys and for lumber to begin the building;
and, before the coming of autumn, laborers and
mechanics were engaged to begin work.

Increasing interest in the project began being
manifested. Time and labor were volunteered:

mechanics with capabilities to perform the work skillfully were hired, and on October 15th, 1877, the corner stone, capping the brick foundation at the north-east corner of the tower, was laid. The ses-

DAVENPORT STREET CHURCH.

sion of the Annual conference had just closed at the Eighteenth street church. and Bishop Bowman with several other prominent clergymen was present; but a driving and chilly rain caused the ceremonies to be abbreviated, much to the disappointment of our people. The plans purposed a one-story frame structure above the foundation, forty-eight by seventy feet, with a prayer and class room in the rear of the main edifice, and a two-story parsonage adjoining. The mechanical work was not let by contract. The pastor assumed the management of the workmen, with the liberal and laborious Richard Stevens as foreman: and, together, they pushed the job vigorously to a finish.

Early in the new year the house was occupied, and services were held in it henceforward; but the dedication was deferred till June 9th, 1878, when Mrs. Maggie Van Cott talked and read the Ritual. The cost of the entire structure was little in excess of $7,900, and was nearly paid for when finished. The statement should not be omitted that the Trustees co-operated with the pastor from first to last: but particularly Mr. Samuel Hawver stood by the work using his own hands nearly all the while in giving assistance to whatever was needing his skill, and, at his own expense, applied the plastering to the walls. The Society again had a place to hold all of its services, and a prospect of holding its place and standing among the religious institutions of the city. The little indebtedness was provided for gradually, as the people recovered from the strain of contributing to the building fund. The old bell was once more put to use by being hoisted to a place in the tower that was provided for it, and for years served to summon the people to church.

During Rev. C. W. Savidge's administration in 1883, the mortgage held by the Church Extension Society was canceled, and, with the accompanying papers, burned in the presence of the congregation, amid demonstrations of thanksgiving that the Society was out of debt! Mr. Savidge organized methods by which he quickly and readily collected the cash that removed the incumbrance, and deserves the credit of having accomplished so desirable an end.

Under the pastorate of Dr. R. N. McKaig, in 1885, the year memorable on account of the evangelical fervor of his preaching and the practical religious life which he taught and exemplified by his own example, as well as the great awakening of the people during a revival at the Exposition Hall, the Church was given an impetus that led to considering the need of a new and better located house of worship. Two lots were purchased of Mr. Frank Murphy at the south-east corner of Twentieth and Davenport streets, at a cost of nearly $9,000 as a beginning; but the Society was timid and did not yet regard itself able to proceed any farther. However the understanding was made public that, when ready, a large central sanctuary would be erected on the lots with a capacity to accommodate the Methodists of the city when they

might assemble for any purpose that should be of
general interest.   It became known to the bishops
that such an enterprise was in contemplation, and
the Society asked for a pastor from abroad who
might bring with him a reputation as a church
builder as well as that he should be an interesting
teacher from the pulpit.

The Superintendents were solicitous that the
right man might be found who successfully would
carry out the program.   Our house now in use had
from neglect become dingy, and its immediate
surroundings offensive.   The people in view of
expecting to be called upon for all the money they
could spare did not care to make any repairs.   A
preacher, Rev. T. M. House, was transferred from
the State of New York, September, 1886, who,
it was expected, would open the campaign and
lead to the consummation devoutly wished.   But
the effort made the following year was not decisive,
though an inconsiderable sum was subscribed;
and any further attempt was delayed till the coming of Bishop Newman to make his home in Omaha
in the fall of 1888.

The bishop perceiving the situation, consulted
the wisest men of the church, called a meeting of
the officers and others in the parlors of the Paxton
hotel, at which he insisted a beginning must be
made, or the meeting place of the General conference of 1892 would most likely be changed.
And, as a further argument, Omaha was much in

need of a prominent church building, centrally located and of an attractive design. These statements wrought an impression on the gentlemen composing the company such that in an hour or two the work was done that set in motion the determining of the question of commencing a structure that would afford sittings for the present and future congregations that might select it as a place of worship, as well as to be an ornament to the part of the city in which it is located.

The preparatory steps were entered upon with earnestness. Expensive drawings and working plans and elaborate specifications were prepared by competent architects, and accepted, with, perhaps, too little knowledge of the sum necessary to complete such a building. Nevertheless, a contract was entered into with Richard Stevens & Son to construct the house and its belongings, except the pews, heating and lighting requisites, and the provision for water for the boiler, organ motor, closets and fountain. The Trustees at this date—S. T. Josselyn, J. H. McConnell, Erastus Young, E. A. Benson, J. B. Carmichael, C. F. Harrison. W. J. Stevens, A. A. McFadden and L. O. Jones—had their hands full in devising the means of prosecuting the enterprise. In April, 1889, a service was held on the site when remarks were made by invited speakers. Drs. Duryea, Lamar and Lemon took part. On the same occasion, the first shovelful of earth was lifted by the president of the

Board of Trustees, Mr. S. T. Josselyn. Immediately excavating for the foundation began, material for commencing the walls was delivered, mechanics went to work, and the scene was animating. Before the lapse of many weeks the basement walls had been raised to the right height to receive the corner stone, which was put in place by the aid of electric lights, after night, July 18th, 1889, with ceremony: on the occasion of which Bishop Newman made an eloquent address just before the dressed ashlar was lowered to its position on the north-west corner of the tower.

But the speedy prosecution of the work was interrupted at intervals from a failure of the factory to furnish the grade of brick required fast enough, and the Church's treasury, in spite of fate, would run empty. The work, however, was allowed only temporarily to stop till the building was enclosed. The great urgency in respect to a more inviting place to worship put the Trustees to their best to reach the point of having the roomy and otherwise superb basement of the new house made ready for occupancy.

On the first day of June, 1890, a farewell meeting was held in the old church, and on Sunday, June 8th, the new basement was opened for services. Bishop Newman was present and preached, and the day was spent in exulting over the success. Money was raised to pay for the furnishings of the several rooms, with what sum Mr. J. O. Phillippi had personally solicited in advance; and in addition some to be used in the further prosecution of the work.

Meanwhile the Trustees negotiated a loan on the old church property of $12,000; and effected a loan of $30,000 of the Northwestern Mutual Life Insurance Company, by mortgaging the new property. Soon as could be, the attention of the mechanics was turned to making ready the auditorium. The arrangement of the room was such as to make progress tedious and difficult, but by dint of persistence, and without encouragement. the contractors kept the work moving through the winter and spring till, on Sunday, May 17th, 1891, the dedicatory program was begun. The services were continued through the week and included the following Sabbath. Either a sermon or lecture was pronounced each week-day evening by ministers of our own or other denominations, and every meeting was an ovation. Bishop Newman preached a discourse on the first Sunday morning to a crowded house, and an appeal for money was made. Dr. B. I. Ives presented the financial condition, and with vehemence pressed a response from the great assemblage. The call for money continued till the last meeting on the program, and the sum of $30,000, the amount sought, was pledged. Bishop Warren was present, by invitation, and preached on the latter Sunday morning, and assisted Bishop Newman in soliciting, and, in the evening, in dedicating the sanctuary.

Never will the people present at these services forget this dedication. The house was in the best of trim, new and clean and bright. All the para-phernalia was in superb order, the acoustics so perfect, and the preaching of the highest order, giving the utmost satisfaction to beholders and auditors!

If the reader is inclined to pursue the story further, a description of the edifice may be inter-esting. as it includes not only the contour but the material of which the walls are constructed, as well as descriptive of internal features: The base-ment walls on the north side and west end are of red sandstone from Portage, Lake Superior, laid in regular courses. On the other side and end the walls are faced from the ground up with red Roman brick. These brick are very hard and will prob-ably never be damaged by age or the weather, and are of unusual size and smoothness. Above the stone work the same brick is used on all sides till the gables are reached, and these and the panels of the tower are laid in ornamental masonry.

The dimensions of the structure are eighty-eight feet frontage on Twentieth street, and ninety-eight on Davenport. The external design is Spanish Romanesque, and while presenting to the eye somewhat of massiveness, the perspective is pleasing and churchly. The tower at the north-west corner rises to the height of one hundred and twenty-five feet, giving a finished appearance to the structure; and, though not elaborate, is symmetrically proportioned in keeping with the edifice of which it is part. The trimmings and copings are of red terra cotta. The cornices and water conductors are copper, as also the jacket covering for about five feet the top of the wall of the lantern surmounting the tower.

The roof is covered with red slate, the peaks of which are coped with copper. The tower is roofed with red Spanish tiling, with a finial of the same material, which, together with the walls, trimmings and main roof presents no feature of color but red.

The entrances to the main audience room and gallery are from Twentieth street, and are approached by substantial stone steps, through heavy double doors swinging outward, and large double doors across the vestibules opening to the auditorium.

The decline in the ground from Twentieth street eastward along Davenport street affords an admirable entrance to the basement near the north-east corner. Inside is an ample vestibule the floor of which, as that of the front lobbies, is laid in a good design of tile. From this floor entrance to the Sunday-school and class-rooms is afforded, or to the audience room and gallery, the ascent to which latter is upon neatly constructed oak stairs; and the ladies' toilet is accessible from a platform in this stairway.

The internal arrangement and finish of the build-

ing are regarded as of superior order. Beginning
with the basement story, which was contrived
for the accommodation of the Sunday-school,
the effect is agreeable. The main room affords
chairs for five hundred. On three sides of this
square are class-rooms separated from the larger
room by sliding doors, so that all of the space of
the lower floor may be in use when occasion
requires except that occupied as a kitchen at one
corner and the library room at another corner.
These apartments are provided with combined
lights of gas and electricity.

Three flights of stairs are provided for reaching
the main audience room from the basement, one
of which leads to the pastor's study on the second
floor as well as the gentlemen's toilet room and the
room containing the organ motor and electric
switches.

Now we are in the main room, and the first sight
impresses the onlooker with the excellence of its
finish, symmetry and completeness of arrangement
throughout. The pulpit and its appurtenances,
the platform, chancel and railing, all of which are
in circular form, are constructed to suit denominational wants, and the mechanism is very complete
and tasty.

The organ loft is in the rear of the pulpit, providing room for the great Boston-made instrument
and the choir. The ascent to this loft, which is
about five-feet above the floor of the altar, is made

by a pair of winding stairs at each side of the pulpit that are mainly concealed from the audience.

The gallery overhanging the outer parts of the audience-room floor makes a circle till it strikes the jambs on each side of the pulpit. It is commodious and affords as comfortable sittings as any other part of the room. From any part of it the hearers can see the preacher, and the speaker is within eyeshot of everybody composing his audience.

The lower floor of the audience room and the gallery are seated with pews, made in circular form and adjusted to the curve of the terrace on which the seats stand. Both the lower and upper floors are inclined toward the pulpit, and bowling, allowing the hearer to overlook those seated in front of him while everybody faces the speaker. The front of the gallery is finished in dado work of quarter-sawed oak, on the face of which is a row of electric lamps, lighting abundantly the space inside of the curve described by the front of the gallery. These two floors will seat more than one thousand, after leaving room for spacious aisles, all radiating from the pulpit as a center and extending from the space outside the altar to the wall aisle that is open on three sides of the room.

The completeness of details in the internal contrivances was secured by the most careful oversight of the superintendent of construction and the vigilance of the Trustees, as well as the interest the contractors took in the work. The structure is in every sense mechanically a substantial house, and was completed at a cost of $86,160, not including the organ, carpets, pews, chairs and gas and electric light fixtures. Adding these, the cost was increased to $99,801, and estimating the real estate, the property is valued at $125,000.

The treasurer of the Board of Trustees, Mr. J. G. Cortelyou, last year, for the purpose of consolidating the debt on the property, secured of the Northwestern Life Insurance Company an additional loan of $20,000, on the same conditions of the former. The interest on the loan and other accruing expenses sums up $10,400 per year. But this burdensome amount is regularly forthcoming, and the Society is making its contributions uncomplainingly.

The history of this old organization that has been perpetuated amid successes and reverses is marvelous beyond any one's ability to rehearse. The intention of putting together the incidents that are here recorded is to present the most cheering along with the least satisfactory occurrences in its long and eventful career. And though there may not now be one of the communicants belonging to the new establishment who worshiped in the first brick meeting house on Thirteecth street, the story is none the less enticing and remarkable.

The large, intelligent and thrifty membership now holding relations to the Society know but

little of the meaning of the conflicts through which
their predecessors had to pass in struggling with
unrest and poverty: but nevertheless have inher-
ited property that descended to their possession,
helping to make more possible the prosperity of
to-day, and are, to that extent, indebted to those
that held the Church together through two or three
decades of varying history.

CHAPTER III.

WITHIN the recollection of a few living citizens Omaha began being built. The plateau between the river and the bluffs had been used since 1850 as a camping ground for companies intending to cross the plains toward California as gold seekers. The Indians were jealous of their rights and would not permit white men permanently to settle and make homes on their soil. Soon after the treaty of June 21st, 1854, between the United States and the aborigines, the level land of the plateau was laid out in lots, which to this date comprises the original City plat, and sales were made at once and buildings erected during the summer and fall. The place was immediately known abroad, and already had a name from its having been visited by so many on their way to the Pacific coast, and from its location on the Missouri which was traversed by steamers carrying passengers and freight to almost every landing on its margin.

Learning of the commencement of a town, the wide-awake itinerant was soon on the spot to open a preaching place to which he might invite the people. There is a claim made, however, that a sermon had been preached on the site of the village before the land was purchased from the Indians, and the dictum comes from high authority, but is as yet without authentication from any other source. Bishop Simpson, in his CYCLOPÆDIA OF METHODISM, states that William Simpson, of the Iowa Conference, who was deputed to do missionary work on the western slope of that State, in 1851 came across the river and preached at Omaha to a few people at the foot of the bluffs. If this be correct, these people must have been stragglers from the caravans on their way to California, and were bivouacked temporarily at this place. In the event of establishing the fact of Mr. Simpson's advent, he must be credited with having preached the first sermon by a Methodist on the west shore of the Missouri north of Kansas.

HISTORY.

The history of the very earliest acts and achievements of the Church must be acquired from the oldest settlers, and as the most of them have ceased to speak, and cannot now be summoned to the bar of truth to affirm or dispute the asseverations of the living, the reason for every statement must be canvassed before crediting it as a verity. The chronicler of events, some of which are but dimly disclosed, must depend in some measure, upon his own ingenuity in presenting them to the student and reader. And but little interest attaches to fumbling and ransacking old and sometimes poorly written reports and records, the inspection of which must be thorough, if the chain of history shall be preserved. But the pleasure of its accomplishment is the incentive to continuing the patience-trying task.

Men who were eager to be the first to lay claim to soil on the west bank of the river had been "waiting and watching" to use the first opportunity. The time came, and the enterprising pioneers began building a town. Among the adventurers was a Methodist preacher, an Englishman of the name of Peter Cooper, who, while yet living at Council Bluffs, was engaged in quarrying stone from a bank south of the present Union Pacific bridge. Upon invitation he made an appointment to preach: and on Sunday, August 13th, 1854, delivered a discourse to an audience of about fifteen persons. The place was at the residence of Wm. P. Snowden, at the corner of Twelfth and Jackson streets. Among the hearers were Mr. and Mrs. Alex. Davis and Alf. D. Jones, the last named leading the singing. Mr. Cooper was not a gifted speaker and made not another appointment. This was the first sermon ever preached in Omaha!

In the spring of 1855 Isaac F. Collins, then a young man, was appointed as a missionary to look after the religious interest of the people of Omaha. Permission was given him to hold services in the old territorial Capitol, and in September following he organized a class of six persons. Mr. Collins perceived the need of having a house dedicated to worship, and projected such an enterprise. The

ferry company, then having control of nearly all
the vacant lots in the village, at the instance of
Mr. A. D. Jones, donated two, equaling one
hundred and thirty-two feet square, to the Methodist Church.   These lots fronted on Douglas
street and were bounded on the east by Thirteenth
street.   With this beginning Mr. Collins proceeded to accomplish still more.   The rear end of
one of the lots was reserved as a site for a church,
and the larger area of the ground was disposed of
and the proceeds were used in procuring materials
for building.   A house about thirty-six feet in
width, facing Thirteenth street, and fifty-eight feet
in length, was begun in the spring of 1856.   The
brisk times of this year were in his favor.   Money
was forthcoming to be employed in the prosecution of the work; and the house was made ready
for occupancy early in the winter, and was dedicated on the sixth of December, 1856, Moses F.
Shinn, officiating.

The walls of the church building were of brick,
one story in height; and the enclosure was all in
one room, with two doors in front and a large, high
window, above which was set in the gable a stone
slab on which was cut "FIRST M. E. CHURCH,
erected 1856."   There were three or four windows
on each side, but none in the west end.   A small
spire was fixed on the top, in which, the next year
after the completion of the house, a bell was hung.
The Society was now pretty well organized for

religious work, with a Sunday-school in operation that secured the interest of the children and young people.

The first Quarterly meeting ever held in Omaha was on September 12th, 1856, William H. Goode, presiding. There were present and partaking of the sacrament on the occasion, Mr. and Mrs. Amsbury, Mr. and Mrs. Collins, Mrs. Crowell, Mrs. McCoy and Mrs. Harris. These persons, probably, comprised the class first organized. It will be noted that this meeting was before the church was ready for use, and was a small beginning.

Mr. Goode was sent from Indiana, and had been selected by the bishops as possessing the courage to make a beginning in a new and unoccupied field, without churches or preachers' houses; and at a time, too, when bands of marauders infested the territory over which he traveled. His authority was that of a Superintendent of the Mission embracing the eastern parts of both Nebraska and Kansas: and the northern portion was temporarily attached to the Iowa Conference, to which he was ordered to report. The opening of this wild region to immigrants invited with others some Methodists whom it was sought to bring under the watchcare of the Church.

The Kansas-Nebraska Annual conference was organized in 1855, and the fourth session was held at Omaha, beginning April 14th, 1859, Bishop Scott in the chair. At this session Hugh D.

Fisher, of the Pittsburg Conference, and Henry T. Davis, of the Northwest Indiana. were announced as transfers. Mr. Fisher was given an appointment in Kansas, and Mr. Davis remained in Nebraska, on which soil he still labors.

Henceforth this new Society was recognized as one of the permanent features of Omaha, and the appointing authorities kept the pulpit of the church supplied. Having now a place of worship it began attracting public attention, and recent accessions to the population of the town steadily increased the size of the congregation. And. it may be. that the encouragement of this kind led to the omission of direct efforts for the salvation of souls, as no mention is made of any religious awakenings.

Mr. Collins had charge for two years, and must have been an industrious worker as is shown by that which was brought to pass. Young as he was when taking charge his youthful zeal and ambition had a chance for full exercise. In the midst of laborious duties he was married to Miss Amsbury, an exemplary young lady, whose parents lived on a farm west of Florence. Within a few years, and after removing to a distant field, she was left a widow at a premature age.

During his term of service at Omaha Mr. Collins was the chief instrument—the managing spirit and business man—in the erection of a house of worship at Florence, at that date the larger town of the two, to which place, after serving Omaha, he was appointed to succeed himself, and served two years, and in the meantime built a parsonage.

These limnings are but echoes of the past about which but few belonging to the great city churches of to-day know anything: but that which was performed in that early day was the beginning of the greater privileges enjoyed by the substantial organizations of the present.

Mr. Goode, the presiding elder, surveyed the field with the eye of an expert, and directed the preachers in his care to the points which in his judgment should have their attention. Looking over the territory adjacent to Omaha on the north, and this side of the Fort, where some families had settled, he took time to canvass the probabilities of its being made a preaching place, and directed Hiram Burch, who labored on a circuit not remote to include this in his plan. Mr. Burch preached at stated times in a school-house in the neighborhood, the site of which was near the present corner of Twenty-fifth street and Ames avenue. A class was organized, and Mr. Goode held a Quarterly meeting for the people interested. But this was not long continued as a meeting place. The attraction of better accommodations and services down town took the attention of those who had been foremost in support of the small class, and their membership was removed.

The management of a charge composed of people from different States and climes, having notions regarding the administration of affairs with which the Church must wrestle as diverse as the dialects of the membership, is usually fraught with more or less annoyance. And, to surmount such obstacles, a pastor and his official members as well as the presiding elder must use good judgment, and, in a measure, overlook the foibles of the erratic. The growth and vigor of the Society in Omaha was held in check while in its crude and formative state, and still under the care of the first pastor and presiding elder, by the course of living of some of its adherents.

Churches on the frontier to whose membership immigrants are being added every week are more likely to be affected with disclaimers than such organizations in old and well-fixed communities. Omaha shared in the affliction of disquieting elements till those who crossed the Missouri came to make permanent homes on her streets, and seeking places of worship where they might rear a reputation for morality and steadfastness in faith, and, though among strangers, find co-workers in the cause of Christ.

Wm. H. Goode remained on the district (his authority as Superintendent of a Mission having been changed to that of presiding elder) till the expiration of four years, and was then transferred to the Conference from which he came. His family was located at Glenwood, Iowa, during his stay in the West, and he was often absent long periods as he traversed the immense field over which he had supervision. While out on one of his rounds his wife died, which added grief to hard work and was enough to break down a man of his age.

John M. Chivington followed Mr. Collins in the pastorate of the Church in Omaha, remaining but one year. Mr. Chivington was not as steady in his demeanor as becomes a man called of God to the work of the ministry, giving his ministerial friends regret and even trouble in their efforts to sustain his reputation. His suavity and ambition secured for him a great influence over men, both strangers and friends; and if his life had with constancy been that of an exemplary man, his usefulness might have been unlimited. Mr. Goode while on his first tour of inspection of the territory found Mr. Chivington in charge of Wyandotte Mission, Kansas, in July, 1854, and was impressed that he should be given work on one of the regular fields under his care; and as a result we learn of his appointment to Omaha as its second pastor.

J. W. Taylor was Chivington's successor as pastor, and served also one year. His membership was continued in the Conference for more than twenty years, and, though never advanced to the best appointments, was always regarded by his colleagues as a trusty and good man. He located in 1862, and afterwards superannuated. But was again made effective, and for several years, and till 1875, his name appears in the list of appoint-

ments. But he again superannuated, and since
which time has been otherwise employed. Mr.
Taylor's ability as a preacher was moderate, but
his soul was full of music, and his voice was strong
and rich in his better days. He now lives in the
north-western part of the State, is growing old, and
is dependent on the Conference fund for part of
his maintenance.

Wm. M. Smith was appointed to the station in
the spring of 1858, and after serving a year was
placed in charge of the Omaha district. Mr.
Smith was a man of good gifts for the pulpit, and
an able manager of the affairs of the Church; but
his sentiments on the question then vexing the
Church and Nation were un-Wesleyan and provok-
ing to a majority of the people comprising the
communicants under his administration. The
membership was small, numbering hardly half a
hundred, and any subject on which they could not
harmonize, and especially the grave one at that
time agitating the commonwealth, was next to a
disaster, as its direct tendency was to hinder the
most successful carrying on of evangelical work.

The bitterness and asperity indulged in mere
conversation were adverse to spiritual growth, and
engendered animosity which has not yet been out-
grown. Mr. Smith's success was not what it
should have been, and, most likely. would have
been, if his views had tallied with a controlling
number of his people. Methodism failed for this

and other reasons to get a prevailing hold on the citizens and, hence, suffered for want of adequate support, either financial or moral.

Henry T. Davis, young and elastic, as well as ready to be placed in the midst of the battle, in the

REV. HENRY T. DAVIS.

spring of 1859 was designated to take charge of the First Church, then regarded as the most prominent appointment in the Conference. At Omaha he finds himself in the Capital of the Territory, a

growing young city full of promise, and to the
far-seeing a field offering a brilliant reward to the
preacher who, under God, might gain access to
the hearts of the people. To be sure there were
prejudices to be overcome and a revolution must
be wrought favorable to Methodism. A steady
and constant effort was needful upon the part both
of the pastor and his people to gain popular confidence; and the house of God must be made more
than usually attractive if public approval and
patronage would be secured.

Mr. Davis with his might began reformatory
efforts, and having some good workers who held
themselves in readiness to assist their pastor in his
attempts to lead men and women to Christ, there
was some good accomplished. The pastor sustained his reputation as seeking not theirs but
them, and at the year's end his return was requested.

Wm. M. Smith now having charge of the Dis
trict, the sentimental disagreements of the previous
year had not been forgotten, but there seemed a
willingness of the membership to forbear, as he
was not so directly concerned in the doings of the
Church as when in the pastoral office. The
preacher-in-charge and the presiding elder entertained reverse views on the absorbing subject
which was also a moral question, but being tolerant,
worked together in the vineyard of the Lord,
though not so amiably as if holding the same opinions. But Mr. Smith's efficiency on the District

carried him in a measure over the head of opposition. And on some charges where he was not well known, by prudently keeping his opinions to himself, he was a popular officer.

The subject that was the cause of the national strife afterwards, now disturbed the people of the Territory the more so because of the agitation growing out of the controversy in Congress and elsewhere over the Kansas-Nebraska bill when it was sought to make of both territories slave soil. The people were more sensitive, perhaps, than the population of the States, and would resent expressions in anywise favorable to slavery.

Mr. Davis was reappointed in 1860 to Omaha, and in earnest entered upon a second twelvemonth's campaign: and before the lapse of another winter rejoiced over a comparatively large addition to the Church, compensating the toil and prayers that had been put forth. This was a great victory, won in the face of almost the worst of antagonism. The pastor had before this turned the advocates of slavery against him by his outspoken utterances and fearless denunciation of the evil. And, besides, his impatient expressions from the pulpit, in remonstrating against popular sins practiced so numerously, brought the opposition of wrong doers. But he steadily pursued a course of conduct that he thought the Head of the Church approved, regardless of fault finders and self-appointed critics.

The returning of Mr. Davis for a second year proved a good thing for himself and the charge, though his allowance was not met. He nevertheless carried away the good will and friendship of the best workers in the charge, and reported fifty additions to the Church.

The Conference was divided, and the northern part thereafter was known as the Nebraska Annual Conference, the first session of which was held in the spring of 1861, at Nebraska City. Omaha was left to be supplied. Three months afterwards David Hart was removed from Calhoun and given charge of the First Church, in the pastorate of which he remained till 1863. His candor and interest in the spiritual well-being of the people attached them to him, and the way was opened for the accomplishment of good.

He came next after Mr. Davis and found two score and more of converts to nurture, as well as all the interests of the charge. His hands and heart had employment, and in the execution of his duties he was faithful. Mr. Hart was humble and devout, wishing only to be used as an instrument in furthering the cause of Christ. He was here at the outbreaking of the Rebellion when conflicting opinions exasperated the public, but he never wavered in his devotion to the work he was sent to do. He held the cross above the American ensign, and courageously pushed the battle of the Lord of hosts :

Though loving his country, while foreign-born he was not much disposed to confer with flesh and blood nor to consume much time in a controversy as to what might result from the contest raging between the North and the South, but was vigilant in seeking the good of men. The Church was in need of a guiding hand, and Mr. Hart's was extended. He made no pretense to being learned in mythology, nor much disposed to giving heed to the conjugation of Greek or English verbs, but, like Paul before Agrippa, could tell his personal and conscious religious experience with good effect, and discourse on the vital things attaching to a holy and consecrated life.

Mr. Hart's second year's labor in Omaha appears to have been nearly fruitless, yet he preserved his integrity and kept the favor of the people. But the increase was nominal, accounted for in a measure by the frequent removals from the city. He ended his labors and life, January 14th, 1878, in Colorado, whence he had gone seeking rest and health. His death was, as might be expected from such a life, triumphant.

Thomas B. Lemon assumed charge of the work the last of March, 1863, and at the same time Isaac Burns was appointed Presiding Elder of the Omaha District—two yoke fellows who could co-operate without any strain or concessions. The popularity of the new pastor nearly insured a harmonizing of the membership as they rallied to his standard of fraternity. The National conflict was rife; but Mr. Lemon refused to commit himself to either side, and with eager desire for success in his charge preached, prayed and sang as if undisturbed by the rigor of fratracidal strife.

REV. THOS. B. LEMON, D.D.

Mr. Lemon was occasionally criticised for his not unreservedly avowing Union sentiments. A story is told that during a session of the Legislature at Omaha after he was elected Chaplain, in a prayer one morning he uttered a petition in behalf of the Chief Executive of the Nation. Some members of the Assembly found fault by saying he did not pray for the country. A lawyer of prominence, and a friend of the Chaplain, told some of them that they were too illiterate to comprehend the meaning of a gifted man's language.

He made friends outside of the Church who voluntarily assisted in the maintenance of the pastor and his projects. The two years of his sojourn in Omaha were almost uninterruptedly pleasant to him and his family, and to the day of his death he had many admirers in the city. Coming to the metropolis at that time, and pursuing the lines of conduct thought by himself the best, he well nigh broke down the partition that separated between the ardent friends of the Government and those who preferred the success of the Confederacy.

At his coming he found nearly a hundred communicants, and received $700 for his first year's allowance. An increase in the number of the membership not worth mentioning is noted at the close of the second year, but his acceptability is signified by his having received on salary, as reported in the Minutes of the Conference, $1.000. and $500 as a donation.

Isaac Burns served two years on the District including Omaha, beginning in 1863. This was long enough to satisfy himself and others that he had but little adaptability to the office, and that the pastoral work was better suited to his gifts and inclination. He was an earnest christian, and his example and precept were more effective when, as a pastor, he was brought into immediate contact with the people. His defect as presiding elder was in his taking little interest in the duties of the office, and hence took no pains to prepare himself, except to preach at quarterly meetings. The latter he enjoyed as an opportunity to reach a great many people, and different congregations every week.

Mr. Burns' health began giving way, and he asked a superannuated relation in 1867, at the session of Conference at Omaha, which relation he sustained for three years, and then accepted from his presiding elder the charge of Nebraska City Mission, which he served for two years. Since 1872 his name does not appear on the Minutes.

Rev. H. T. Davis in his book, "Solitary Places made Glad," in speaking of his death says: "Isaac Burns was a simple-minded, conscientious, sweet-spirited and deeply pious man. * * * One always felt benefited spiritually by being in his company." He is now numbered with the crowned ones.

Wm. M. Smith was returned to the charge in in 1865, after the lapse of about six years since his former pastorate. Omaha was a village when he served the Church at an earlier date, now it claims as its population four thousand souls, and no less of a change in the congregation was apparent. He reached the city in time to preach on the Sabbath following the assassination of President Lincoln. The church was draped, and loyal men and women were in mourning as if one of their own household had been taken away. They were in expectation that a memorial service would be held. Mr. Smith entered the pulpit at the appointed hour, and to many present was not a stranger. He chose as a text I Cor. ii, 2: "For I determined not to know anything among you, save Jesus Christ, and him crucified," and proceeded to preach. In the discourse he made no allusion either to the preparation of the room for the occasion nor to the taking off of the now dead Chieftain, totally ignoring the sad and disappointed people who had met to honor his name and to do a most willing part in perpetuating a remembrance of his noble manhood and distinguished patriotism.

Mr. Smith was not willing to concede that he made a mistake in paying no respect to the feelings or preferences of a large share of the people present; but the loyal and patriotic at once decided not to sustain a man, though appointed as a pastor, who would so brazenly offer an affront! A few weeks later the Quarterly conference met, and after proceeding with the business till the question was reached, "What has been raised for the support of the ministry this quarter?" Answer: "Nothing!"

The presiding elder, who was present and in the chair, was informed that on condition he would remove the offending pastor, he would receive pay for the time he had served; otherwise he would get no salary. He was removed, and for a time the charge was left pastorless. Mr. Smith's name appears not again in the Minutes as a pastor, but as having superannuated. He removed to Colorado and it is intimated became connected with the M. E. Church, South: and now owns and lives upon a ranch a few miles west of Pueblo in that State.

W. B. Slaughter was Mr. Smith's successor, and supplied the pulpit of the First Church till the close of the year after the dismissal of the latter in the summer of 1865; and was reappointed to the charge in 1866 and the year following. This was Mr. Slaughter's first ministerial work in Nebraska. He brought scholarship and experience as well as devotion and pressed them into service, attracting to his ministry the thoughtful and best cultured people of the city. His previous habits of reading, study and thought had provided him with a fund of information that was now available to him, and interesting to his hearers, and both he and they were flattered with the prospects.

The Methodist Church was now the place of entertainment on the Sabbath, and, as a consequence, the congregation much the largest in the city. The up-building suggested the need of a

better church house, and a good deal of talk was
indulged in respecting such an undertaking. The
times were brisk, the city was spreading, and all
things combined calling for keeping pace with the
town in church enterprise. But he faltered not in

REV. WM. B. SLAUGHTER, D.D.

his endeavors to instruct the people from the pulpit, and many new friends came to the support
of the Church. Mr. Slaughter's practical yet
scholarly method of presenting truth rarely failed
of eliciting commendation. But the subject of

better accommodations in the house of God was troublesome.

Mr. Slaughter himself was sanguine, and partook of the spirit of bettering the privileges of church-goers. Propositions were made and considered. but for some time no decisive steps were taken. All branches of trade were feeling the impulse, and his people began growing restless, and, it may be, a little vain, in desiring to be better fixed as to a place of worship. The old edifice that had been hastily constructed and without ornaments, was not after the style of new buildings going up on the principal streets, business was encroaching upon the site of the church, and in the opinion of the best judges something must be done, and done speedily—no time must be wasted in parleying.

Mr. Slaughter, seizing the opportunity, was enabled to report the largest number of probationers that had ever been counted in this charge in any pastoral term, and he received the largest salary ever paid to a pastor up to that date.[*]

Thomas B. Lemon was Mr. Slaughter's presiding elder, and the Church felt that it was greatly favored in having so much talent as was possessed in the brains of these veteran itinerants. They together were the strongest dual in the Conference. Mr. Lemon's administration on the District was

---

[*] On another page the reader may learn what was done.

in advance of his predecessor as much as to be noticeable wherever he presided in a Quarterly conference. Under him, and by his scrutiny of the fitness of the preachers manning the several charges, and his able counsels in the management of the field, as well as the influx of population, the District was immensely improved during the four years of his term.

Methodism in these parts owes a debt of gratitude to these two men's effective work that it has never discharged, and of which it was not conscious at the time of their rendering the great service. * And if its advancement had been continued, long since it would have been dominant in the city and the region adjacent. The hurt from backsets cannot now be retrieved, but it has measurably recovered the disappointment.

Henry C. Westwood, transferred from the Baltimore Conference, was next in the succession of pastors. He arrived in May, 1865, more than a month after the closing of Mr. Slaughter's term. The agitation the year before of the project of more inviting quarters as a place of worship resulted in the quitting of the old church and making expensive alterations in the structure that it might be rented as a source of revenue. The congregation had already hired and had begun

* Both are deceased, having ended their days and labors in this city.

using the German Methodist church as a place of
meeting.　Mr. Westwood's cultivated notions of
propriety were almost shocked at the coarse looking
apartments of this cheap building: and as a con-
cession to his wishes the Trustees hired the privi-

REV. H. C. WESTWOOD.

lege of using the Academy of Music as a preaching
place only once a week—on the Sabbath.

　Mr. Westwood reports having large congregations, and that the Official Board and himself were

in complete harmony. The Estimating Committee suggested $2,000 as his salary, and the Quarterly conference confirmed their judgment. A new and comfortable parsonage housed him and his family, and the prospect was flattering. The thoughts of the official members were much engrossed in devising a method by which money might be secured to provide a new chapel. Mr. Westwood interested himself in giving assistance, to the partial neglect of more directly religious work. The congregation was not held to the maximum; no revival occurred, though the preacher failed not to be in the pulpit on Sunday. But before the winter was ended, and while the new chapel's walls were being raised, there were intimations of discontent.

The pastor did not enjoy western etiquette nor the bland manner of some of his parishioners. Much of his former life had been spent among better polished people, and he hardly would tolerate those who could not appear well at their homes or in society; and he almost refused to visit the humble poor of his charge. Nothing better might be expected than that fault-finders would use such an opportunity to complain of the pastor. There seemed to be but little room left for mutual good feeling between the servant and the served, and before the ending of the first year the chances for the accomplishing of good were lost.

Mr. Westwood was, in appearance, an accomplished gentleman, and an interesting sermonizer. His efforts in the pulpit were not criticised unfavorably; and if he had not persisted in his exhibitions of an haughty spirit, accepting the situation in right good fellowship, he might have been very certainly a useful man in Omaha. As it was, he went to Conference under a cloud, pursued by a delegate from his charge instructed to ask for his removal. But he was reappointed only to meet such opposition as forced his presiding elder, A. G. White, to consent to his removal in three months. He was transferred to the Conference which he left to come west. His death occurred at Fredonia, N. Y., August, 1890.

Moses F. Shinn, in those days a handy man to use in filling a gap, and having reformed, was employed to take charge till some one might be secured permanently to stand in his stead as pastor. Mr. Shinn was a man of much experience in the ministry, and, at times, of great value to the Church. He was a cheerful companion, and a speaker of no mean qualities, sound in doctrine and a thoroughly orthodox Methodist.

Alvin G. White, in 1869, was made presiding elder of the Omaha District. He had been a member of the Conference since his admission in 1863; and takes charge of the district work in the prime of manhood, and a little elated at the sudden promotion and the authority vested in him by this appointment. But his capabilities were unquestionably equal to the honor, as he was educated, a preacher of good gifts and a versatile writer, studious, discriminating, sensible and vivacious, making himself familiar with his subject before presenting it to the public. He failed not to edify a promiscuous congregation, securing without much exertion a respectful hearing.

He had admirers among the membership, and was encouraged by their good opinions of him and his excellent service. But he may have been too sensitive over criticisms of small things that were not in keeping with the notions entertained of him by his friends, and would fret and become petulant. He remained the full term of four years, and witnessed the Churches on the District growing steadily in numbers and influence.

The Society had recently occupied the new chapel on Seventeenth street, and there was a prevailing opinion among the worshipers, that a preacher of sterling qualities was needed for the pulpit. A small sum was spent in telegraphing the bishop having jurisdiction and others as they sought the right man. Six weeks were consumed in the canvass before an announcement of success could be made. But a man of commanding presence and ability was selected, in the person of Gilbert De La Matyr, who, upon his coming, was not disappointing, but, the rather, was received with great favor, and at once was acknowledged as the right man.

Mr. De La Matyr was a transfer, and for this reason was regarded by older Methodist pastors with a little jealousy. Indeed it had become a rule that the First Church must have a preacher for its

REV. GILBERT DE LA MATYR.

pulpit of such reputation as none in the Conference possessed; and for this reason stood almost alone and without sympathy from pastors outside of the city. Whatever of detriment may have come from this source could hardly be avoided, as church-goers made the demand. And if the pulpit had not been manned with the equal of other city pastors. many would forsake the congregation and go else-where for entertainment.

The new pastor's austere appearance and rare ability might have kept the people aloof: but his kind heart and affability soon assured them that he could get down and receive them as humbly and cheerfully as if they were akin. Exhibitions of mutual appreciation were soon apparent, and almost from the outset every indication was favorable. He was a western man and had no trouble in adjusting himself to the conditions as he found them, as he philosophically took in by his good sense all the surroundings and made the best of them.

But his strength in the pulpit was the winning feature. He was systematic, clear and argumen-tative in discoursing, clothing his thoughts in pure English, often making striking illustrations. His classic language was pleasing to the ear, and his application sent the truth home. His stentorian voice was not an objection for he did not often use it in its full power, but held it under control. In his best days he was one of the most finished and able preachers in the West, attracting the lovers of good sermons till he had a congregation that was envied by others, which he maintained, through three years of unremitting service in numbers and quality. When, in 1872, his term expired Methodism was erect and aggressive, having entirely met its obligations and pledges to the public.

Mr. De La Matyr fell at his post about two years since at Akron, Ohio, greatly lamented by a host of friends.

In its evolutions the itinerant wheel brought Geo. W. Gue to the pastorate of the mother church in the spring of 1872. His predecessor's having enjoyed success without interruption for nearly three years, laid upon him a load that was enough to make him anxious. Expectation was not easily nor quickly met, and the incoming pastor keenly felt the demand on him. But in good spirit he opened the campaign while the Church was flushed with victory, and with persistence and fervor kept the record good. The Sunday-school was an auxiliary in advancing the interests, and, co-working, was a great factor in the Church.

Mr. Gue was a man of genuine piety desiring the greatest good to the largest number. His pleasing address and genial cheerfulness helped him to be generally acceptable in the pastoral office. If he had been measured alone by his erudition or his expertness in punctuating his deliverances, his acceptability would not have been so general nor his pastorate so heartily approved. He was small of stature, though stout, quick in movement and busy, and had a helpful word for every one.

His presiding elder, A. G. White, at the end of the year's work reported of him that. "he labored faithfully and gained the confidence and affections of the people. Unfortunately he had become surety for a friend and was involved to such an

REV. GEORGE W. GUE.

extent as to embarrass him in feelings and labor; and that he might relieve himself, accepted a lucrative position, resigning the charge a few weeks ago."

Under date of August 2d, 1894, Mr. Gue writes:

"My year among the Omaha people was a very pleasant experience. I was kindly received, and throughout the term was treated with the greatest christian courtesy. But there was no revival nor any special religious interest to make my pastorate remarkable among them."

Mr. Gue is now presiding elder of Portland district, Oregon.

A new pastor and presiding elder now take charge of the work, in the persons of Clark Wright and Geo. W. De La Matyr, both of whom were lately transferred from other Conferences, and who, as yet, unacquainted with western life, were scrutinized by the churchmen with the utmost care in determining their fitness.

Mr. Wright with confidence took hold of the work in the spring of 1873, and finding that he would meet little, if any, difficulty growing out of the popularity of the man whom he followed, brought all his resources into use and was soon on the way to encouraging success. His first year was lengthened by a change in the time of the meeting of the Annual conference from spring to fall. This was no detriment to him nor the Church, and only served to unite more closely, by longer acquaintance, the bond of fellowship between the pastor and his people. He was efficient both in the pulpit and out of it to the extent of winning the favor of both old and young.

The Sunday-school, under the ingenious man-

agement of Samuel Burns, had attained remarkable success, and really controlled the suffrages of
a large number of the church people, among them
the ablest officers and teachers. In the spring of
1874, and when Mr. Wright had been in charge

REV. CLARK WRIGHT.

one year, there occurred a troublesome menace
both to the Church and school. Mr. Burns' success and popularity aided in his insisting that
nothing should be allowed to interrupt his method

of conducting the school or the weekly teachers' meetings.

But withal there was a disposition on the part of the Society to overlook such foibles, till Mrs. Van Cott, the Evangelist, then at her best, was invited to Omaha to hold a meeting in connection with the First Church in the interest of holiness. She received, as might be expected. the endorsement of the pastor and Official Board, but her manner and method soon became displeasing to Mr. Burns, though at the first he took part in the services.

Mrs. Van Cott is liable to be accused in conducting services of being vain and conceity. This, together, with the favoritism of Mr. Wright and her domineering manner in demanding the discontinuance of some of the sessions of the Sunday-school, provoked a conflict setting the Evangelist and Superintendent at variance. But a little later, and after the revival meeting had attracted a larger attendance and begotten an increasing religious interest, she appointed. as was her custom, prayer and band meetings for the soul culture of all who wished to avail themselves of such privileges, and insisted upon a prompt and general daily attendance. Mr. Burns suspected an interference directly with the school, and did not prefer to submit.

These extraordinary services once or twice a week came in the way of Mr. Burns' mid-week meeting for Bible study or encroached upon his hour for Sunday-school, though he made some move to prevent a conflict of appointments. Mrs. Van Cott's resolute obstinacy would not suffer any antagonism, and she unhesitatingly rebuked any attempt to carry on any other services while hers were in progress.

Mr. Burns resented the disposition to dictate what he should do, and the Evangelist's friends— of whom she had not a few—defended her course. This brought about so great unpleasantness between the organized school and the Official Board as to threaten a rupture of the Church, which, in a short time, resulted in the asking for certificates of dismissal by Mr. Burns and his friends. The Official Board refused the use of the chapel for the school and it was withdrawn, and began holding its sessions in the Presbyterian church across the street.

Mr. Wright could not avoid participating in the controversy. He favored Mrs. Van Cott while deploring the occurrence, but could see no way out of the trouble except by a separation of the discordant elements. Twenty-four of the membership asked for and received certificates, and a large share of the Sunday-school and most of the teachers followed Mr. Burns. Before the next session of the Annual conference the disaffected members—Burns, Homan, Steele, Hills, Garrison, Marston, Parmalee, Whitmore, Arnold, and their wives, and Mrs. McCoy and others—had provided a place to meet. *

Mr. Wright was re-appointed in October, 1874, and summoning his best strength and help endeavored to make good the loss. The number recruited from the world in Mrs. Van Cott's meeting nearly doubled the former membership, the most of whom remained with the First Church. And with Hawver, McKoon, Frost, Roberts, Tousley, Lange, Webster, McLain, Downs and others remaining he had a corps of good and willing workers, who, with their wives, gave such sustenance as to set in motion the old Church: and a reorganization of the Sunday-school was soon effected, giving the appearance of a thrifty and progressive Society.

Mr. Wright ended the second year's service having the favor of the people. He had preached with acceptability, managed the affairs of the Society in a manner that was commendable, received his salary and accepted a transfer to Montana. He reported a membership before leaving of 295, and a Sunday-school of 240.

Mr. De La Matyr, the presiding elder, was not merely a spectator while the irritating disturbance was pending, in which, at the outset, Mr. Burns and Mrs. Van Cott were the combatants in chief, and which led nearly all the membership to take

*See elsewhere a description of the place.

sides, but he was solicited to adjudicate some
points in the controversy which lasted several
months. Attempts were frequently made in the
Quarterly conference to bring about a reconcili-
ation. The presiding elder was in the chair, but
his counsel was construed as favoring Mr. Burns.
Thereafter his official services were not acceptable
to the First Church; and, indeed, the officers would
have preferred his non-attendance.

He, however, was a worthy man, and his inten-
tions were doubtless right. As a pulpit man his
strength was not great enough to overcome much
opposition. In social circles he was reserved and
did not appear cordial. During his term of thirty
months he did not succeed in attracting the people
to him as a heroic and eloquent man could have
done, and had to forfeit his place. He and Mr.
Wright retired from laboring in this city at the
same time.

Leroy F. Britt, in 1875, as pastor, and Henry T.
Davis, as presiding elder, together took the First
Church under their administration. They both
had families and lived in the city. The Society
now enjoyed relief from the parties concerned in
the strife of a year before, and were ready to affil-
iate with the incoming officers.

Mr. Britt labored with zeal till winter, and,
with the aid of reliable lay helpers, was instrumental in promoting a revival during which about
seventy were added to the Church. Once a week

all the year through the praying Band, such as
Mrs. Van Cott inaugurated, met and held service
consisting of exhortation, prayer and testimony.
The fervency and spirit with which this meeting
was carried on was a great help to the pastor in
keeping devotion alive. Mr. Britt's health nearly
failed in the spring, crippling his work for the

REV. LEROY F. BRITT, D. D.

remainder of the year, till, excepting the revival,
he was unable to accomplish much.

In the pulpit Mr. Britt was practical in enforcing truth upon his hearers, and sometimes a little
vehement. His vocalization was heavy, and he
could command a hearing by the strength of his

voice. His efforts frequently partook of the form of exhortation, and he enjoyed more this manner of enforcing truth than by presenting arguments or discussing points of doctrine. He almost wholly rejected theories, and sought facts of experience.

At this juncture in the old Church's history not an unexpected embarrassment presented itself. However certainly it had been anticipated, it came nevertheless as the shock of an avalanche. All of the property of the Church had been mortgaged, and was now liable to forfeiture. The uneasiness begotten of this state of affairs was overwhelming; and on canvassing the matter no way could be devised by which the calamity might be averted. But by the clemency of the bondholders an agreement was effected between them and the Trustees that the Society might use the church and parsonage for a few months beyond the limit, on condition of a voluntary surrendering of all right, title and interest to the property on Thirteenth and Seventeenth streets at the expiration of that time. The value of this, including real estate and buildings, was not far from $50,000.

Thus the case remained till Mr. Britt's year closed, and he was removed to another field. He is now a presiding elder in the Nebraska Conference and is doing effective service.

The Presiding Elder, H. T. Davis, with the experience of twenty years in the ministry, was no

novice in the execution of clerical duty. Neither
was this his first work on a District, but he had a
disciplining elsewhere in this office, preparing him
the more readily to put the machinery in motion.
He neglected nothing in his line, and for two
years labored assiduously in building up the
Churches in his field.

Dr. Hugh D. Fisher appeared upon the scene
as a new pastor, October, 1876, just in time to
wrestle with an emergency that was pending and
seemed inevitable. The pulpit at the late session
of the Conference had been left to be supplied.
The Bishops had been advised as to the precarious
situation of the business connected with the
property of the First Church; and were equally well
apprised that, if anything might be accomplished,
the charge was in need of an experienced leader
in whom preaching and business ability combined
in no small measure. Dr. Fisher at this time
was laboring in Cincinnati, and, hearing the appeal
of the Bishops, consented to come to the relief of
a Church that was likely to become bankrupt.
His arrival was welcomed by the leading men of
the charge, and he immediately began work with
his accustomed and tireless energy.

He inspected every feature of the dilemma with
the sagacity of an adept, not only to ascertain if
any compromise might be made with the bondholders, but as to the willingness and ability of the
people whom he served to give substantial aid.

The membership generally had small, if any, bank
accounts; and the farther he carried his inquiries
the more dubious he became of success in saving
the property; and, finally, relinquished the trial as
useless.   Making the matter still worse, the people

REV. HUGH D. FISHER, D.D.

had only begun recovering from the grasshopper
scourge of the year before which had temporarily
impoverished the southern and western parts of
the State, in which calamity the city shared in no

small degree. The Trustees, hence, could not do otherwise than surrender all the possessions of the Church, though permitted to use the chapel till the first of July, 1877.

Dr. Fisher by this time had gained in the esteem of citizens as well as of the Society so much as to call out large congregations to his ministry. The seriousness of the case with which he had been dealing was not enough to daunt him, and he courageously kept up his efforts in behalf of the charge. The Masonic Hall at the corner of Sixteenth street and Capitol avenue was rented, after vacating the chapel, and the services were held in that room till mid-winter.

In the meantime the indefatigable pastor, by the help of the Trustees, had planned and begun the construction of a new house of worship which was soon afterwards finished and used.* After the occupancy of the new house, and as long as he remained in authority, the attendance at the Sabbath services was fully maintained, though a little dissatisfaction had grown out of his impatient and petulant habits.

The Doctor in the pulpit always commanded respect. In him was no trifling before an audience; and the strong and manly presentation of the subject of discourse was always creditable to his head and heart. His argumentation was logical

---

* It is described in another chapter.

and scriptural. and discerning the points himself, they were made transparent to his hearers. To sum it up, he was no ordinary teacher of the great things of the gospel, but luminious and earnest, he made his sermons attractive and helpful.

In stature the doctor was tall, erect and slender. In movement agile and alert, possessing great power to endure fatigue. He was never overloaded with work, but had such a facility for accomplishing that he kept his study table clear, and his outside duties up to date.

He served nearly three years, did an immense amount of work, and was transferred to Salt Lake City a few weeks before Conference to take charge of our denominational work at that place.

Dr. W. B. Slaughter served as presiding elder the last two years of Dr. Fisher's pastorate; a man of strong thought, and a methodical preacher; a divine of large and increasing acquaintance with men of literature and clergymen of note. He was likewise a writer of ability, clear, concise and analytical. If he had lived a few years longer most likely would have written and published a History of Methodism in Nebraska for which he was already collecting matter.

His labors were cut short in the midst of usefulness by a violent attack of sickness resulting in death at his home in West Omaha, July 26th, 1879, before the close of his second year on the Omaha District. Bishop Andrews was summoned from

Des Moines to preach at his funeral, attending which a large congregation assembled at the First Church, where in his life time he was wont to preach the gracious gospel, and which charge he had served long since as pastor.

REV. JOHN B. MAXFIELD, D. D.

Dr. J. B. Maxfield, in 1879, having just retired from the North Nebraska District, became the pastor of this Church. He was well known, and himself knew well the situation of a charge he had frequently heard represented in the Cabinet. This acknowledgment of his fitness saved the transportation of a supply from outside of the Conference. He easily adjusted himself to the work, though he had been a series of years laboring in another department.

The legitimate duties of a pastor only were to be performed: a church and a parsonage had been built by his predecessor, giving him an open field and a fair chance. All the business annoyances and unwieldy debts had been disposed of till the Society was now feeling comparatively easy. But the Church was without wealth or patrimony, and of slow growth, as the most of the accessions were by letter, yet it was able to give the pastor a living salary.

Shortly after taking charge, Pastor Maxfield began reading his sermons from the pulpit. Those who had heard him preach without using a manuscript to trammel him, protested in moderation, and he desisted, much to the pleasure of the congregation. He never failed to enlighten his hearers on the subject in hand nor to edify his people. With him in the pulpit the assurance that the services would be interesting was not doubtful: and he was able to hold this good opinion and respectful hearing to the end of his labors in the charge. Closing the second year as pastor he was removed to take charge of the Omaha District.

Dr. W. G. Miller, a transfer from the Wisconsin Conference, was appointed to the District in 1879, succeeding Dr. Slaughter, and, remaining only two years, was removed to take charge of York District now, and since the division, in the Nebraska Conference. In this latter, he labored on Districts till 1892, when age forbade his longer continuance in active service. His decease ocurred December 20th, 1893, at University Place, near Lincoln, at the age of 71.

Dr. Miller was one of the foremost, most effic-ient and popular preachers of Wisconsin, and was always in demand for the best positions. His best work was not all wrought from the pulpit; but he was kind, generous and careful in his behavior toward others, which was reciprocated by his ministerial brethren; and he was always a favorite in the households of his charge.

In his best days Doctor Miller had superior qualities for the office of Presiding Elder, as well as excelling in the pastorate. His executive ability was of high order, enabling him to dis-pose of the most difficult matters with the greatest facility and ease. His cordial and unselfish heart attracted men to him, and his affability secured their permanent friendship.

As a preacher he was a model in persuasiveness, and, hence, almost irresistible when discoursing upon matters of duty. He never aimed to give prominence to his learning, and was not in the habit of announcing mechanical divisions of his sermons, yet the line of argument was none the less distinct. His public efforts were full of the marrow and· fatness of the gospel, by reason of which traits he was a soul-winner of unusual success.

REV. J. W. STEWART.

In the pastorate of the First Church, J. W. Stewart was the next in succession, assuming charge September, 1881. He labored from the first with eager desire to promote the interests of pure religion in this city. His ardent and consistent piety gave him a strong hold of the more devout of his people; but, for the same reason, others were inclined to find fault. And the disinclination of the latter to give sustenance, among them the usually most liberal supporters with their money, really led to his removal at the first year's end.

Mr. Stewart was a revivalist in a large sense, and his preaching, in the main, was after the style of an evangelist, searching and forceful. And with such encouragement as he deserved he would have accomplished the bringing in of many souls to the Kingdom and the Church. This, as he perceived, was the want of Methodism in Omaha, hence the pressing of the subject from his pulpit.

He much preferred the practical religious life, and he seldom presented any other character of theme; and, for this reason, was thought to be unable to discourse upon current and developing questions of biblical study and criticism.

C. W. Savidge, a transfer from Minnesota Conference, was the succeeding appointee to the pastorate. In the fall of 1882 he came as a stranger, young, active, unmarried, and yearning to be useful. The impression on the people was not favorable at the outset; embarrassed in appearing before a new congregation turned his attention from himself, and his posing was neither graceful nor clerical. But he overcame his critics by his ceaseless interest in his work and his zeal in prosecuting it.

In the pulpit Mr. Savidge was not what is understood as profound; but he was an interesting talker. Something fresh and novel was always enunciated, without repetition of any former utterance. It was not his habit so much to examine a

REV. CHAS. W. SAVIDGE.

subject for discussion as to find something to say that would interest his hearers. He appropriated the daily occurrences and scenes met with in his rounds of visiting, and applied them to good advantage in preaching.

As a rule, he wrote his sermons pretty fully,

but did not use his manuscript in the pulpit. He has been known to hand his written sermon to a reporter, and then deliver the discourse as it would appear the next morning in a daily, having been set from his manuscript.

He was noted for his promptness. No work was undertaken by the church except he participated. When the bell had ceased ringing for services either on the Sabbath or week day he was in his place and ready. If he were summoned to a funeral or invited to dine at a fixed hour, he never failed of being on time. And his preparation for the pulpit was matured and ready for delivery when the occasion came. When he made a call he did not forget the injunction to spend no more time than necessary; and he always had something pending. In a word, he was constantly engaged, and never triflingly employed. In a report to the second Quarterly conference, January 26th, 1884, Mr. Savidge writes: "Since the date of October 29th, 1883, I have preached twenty sermons to the congregation and ten to the children. I have made one lecture and three addresses; and have made two hundred pastoral calls, and officiated at seven funerals," etc.

During the winter season he would make search for the needy and provide relief. It is related that when the housekeeper one morning was dressing his room provided with his own furnishings, she missed the blankets from his bed. On asking about them, he said he found a destitute family and had carried them away.

Mr. Savidge was a good solicitor of money for the Church. When the house in which he preached was built, a loan of $3,000 was effected from the Church Extension Society to run several years. Nothing had been applied on the principal up to date, and it was nearly due. He organized methods to get money, and readily secured it all and more.

The Church was built up under his admistration till it could take care of itself and its pastor. After serving successfully the limit of three years, he was appointed to Seward street Church in this city.

J. W. Phelps, late of the Rock River Conference, was appointed to the Omaha District in 1885. as Dr. Maxfield's successor, and at the same time of the accession of R. N. McKaig to the pastorate of the First Church.

Mr. Phelps was an able preacher, having a strong and impressive voice and an oratorical delivery. He was a man of pleasing address and a good friend of his preachers. His management of the District was creditable to himself and the Church. He was on intimacy with Bishop Fowler, whose residence at that time was in San Francisco, who planned for the removal of Mr. Phelps to the Pacific coast. He spent two years on the District and was in the midst of the third when the way was opened for him to go. Quitting the District, he speedily made ready to leave Nebraska, and the District was turned over to T. C. Clendening, then serving as pastor of South Tenth street Church.

Dr. R. N. McKaig had just ended a pastoral

REV. ROBERT N. McKAIG, D.D.

term at Lincoln, Nebraska, and was transferred from that Conference to this, in September, 1885, and was stationed at the First Church, Omaha. His services were sought for Wabash Avenue

Church, Chicago; and the disappointment of his being removed to this city, instead, was not satisfactory to him, though he obediently submitted. On his arrival at the Omaha depot, brethren with carriages met and wheeled him and his family to the parsonage, where the ladies had spread a palatable luncheon. His fame had preceded him, and the Church people anticipated a year of great things. The beginning was full of promise and continued to be encouraging. Winter came, and he began holding frequent services intended to build up the membership in spiritual life. A little later an Evangelist was called to his assistance. The revival brought out large gatherings, among them many ungodly.

The awakening of the city was his object, and he insisted upon the hiring of Exposition Hall that ample room might be provided. After considering the enormous expense that must be incurred by removing to the Hall, the officers of his Church consented. The result, whether justifying the removal or not, was almost like a panic. A great many were taken into the Church both of saved and unsaved. The good done will not be revealed till the great day of assize!

Dr. McKaig's faith and zeal were wonderful, and he desired a fair chance to test what God would do in answer to prayer from a heart all burdened for the salvation of the people; and while his brethren at first remonstrated to the

change of place of meeting, he spent a great deal
of time on his knees pleading with God to change
their mind, and he prevailed.

He was faithful to his calling as if he were
responsible for the souls of all in his hearing.
There was no intermission in his endeavors to do
good. In his preaching he insisted upon pure
lives and exact living by pointing out the way to
heaven so distinctly that he could not be misunder-
stood. He believed the Scriptures to be a revela-
tion of the will of God to man, and sought to lead
others to accept them as a boon to the fallen race.

As a preacher he excelled in fervency; and as a
teacher of the Word his language was indicative
of great confidence in what he taught. His sermons were radiant with the beauty of the christian
life. He prepared for the pulpit in the closet, and
then disclosed his burning thoughts to his auditors,
as if his soul were on fire of the gospel theme! In
the application he was singularly impressive and
happy. But he was not a monomaniac, nor did
he claim for himself that degree of purity that
exceeded the grace enjoyed by his fellows.

As a share of the result of his work, his report
of the date of May 17th, 1886, will exhibit in a few
words: "Received by letter, seventy; received on
probation, two hundred and eighteen. I have
visited all the families of the Church, at least,
once; and have called on nearly two hundred
families outside. The Church has been progress-

ing in spiritual power, and we are now confident in the Lord that we shall have a revival all the time."

During the year two lots were purchased at the south-east corner of Davenport and Twentieth streets, as a site for a greatly-needed new house of worship, and about $3,000 applied in payment.

Shortly before the close of his first year's service, Dr. McKaig was offered and accepted the presidency of our Seminary at York, without notifying his Church of his intention. This, of course, removed him from this charge to the regret of a great many of his friends.

Succeeding to the pastorate next was T. M. House, who was transferred, September, 1886, from the State of New York to inaugurate the new church enterprise. In the opinion of the Bishop having jurisdiction he was the right man, and he was expected to bring things to pass accordingly. The subject was mooted now and then, but nothing favorable, much less encouraging, was done. The pastor was willing to make the attempt, but could not prevail upon the Official Board and particularly the Trustees to agree that the time had come. After spending about two years in charge he opened a subscription and obtained the promise of several thousand dollars, but not a sum such as to give assurance or even a prospect of success. Finding himself unable to manage the case the whole matter was delayed till the arrival of Bishop Newman in the autumn of 1888.

The above statement is confirmed by an item in the Journal of the Quarterly conference of the date of October 18th, 1888:

"Bishop Newman having been with us during the past two weeks taking the initiative in raising subscription for the

REV. T. M. HOUSE.

new church building, is meeting with success; $24,000 have been subscribed, and it is hoped in another week it will be raised to $30,000.

F. W. HILLS, Sec'y.　　T. C. CLENDENING, P. E."

Mr. House, probably, had little adaptability to pastoral duties, and the Society did not hold its own under his administration. The directly religious features of the work were in a measure neglected, as also the visiting from house to house, till, in his report to the Annual conference, at the end of his term, the figures show a large falling off in numbers. He gave attention, chiefly, to preparation for the pulpit, and the other duties of his office were subordinated to this.

In the pulpit Mr. House was able and interesting. He fully wrote his sermons in his study, and read them verbatim from the desk. His gifts in composition were more than equal to his eloquence of delivery, but his sermons were appreciated as literary productions of real merit, pleasing to the ear and enchanting to the listener. And, if he had maintained the good will of all the membership, the three years of his serving would have been reckoned a success.

T. C. Clendening now having charge of the District went to work with restless activity. Every charge, pastor, church and parsonage building was scanned with care, and the outlying regions were not neglected. Perhaps the whole field has never had better oversight than was given it under his faithful and diligent management. He wearied not in the more than five years of superintendency, and, closing his term, left the District in good condition for his successor.

He was instrumental in either the organization or building up of suburban charges in the margin of Omaha, some of which are now self-sustaining and promising. And in rural and hitherto neglected parts, adjacent to country circuits, he advised that such places be included in the work. Before the reverses in the times began making an impression on the money market and the public, he was very active in starting the building of country churches and parsonages, some of which are now dedicated or occupied.

P. S. Merrill came next in the succession of pastors of the First Church, arriving in September, 1889. His transferring from Philadelphia gave some assurance that he could lead and would serve with ability. He accepted the appointment and transfer with the understanding that the new church enterprise had been undertaken, and that as a servant of the Church he would be expected to employ his working skill to the best advantage.

The erection of the building was a venture. The preparatory work, so far as obtaining subscription, was not a guarantee that it could be completed. This placed him in an unenviable predicament soon as he made the first movements. He could discern that the house would be finished and furnished only by the utmost exertions of all concerned in the management of the business. Money was advanced as the people were pressed, and there was need of an experienced solicitor and collector.

The Trustees were business men, but their own affairs engaged their time so much that they reluctantly gave attention to the building. This

REV. PHILIP S. MERRILL, D. D.

imposed too much on the pastor, who was taking his first lessons in architecture, and he in a measure failed in getting money. The work was carried on, however, through the winter of 1889, and at

the opening of the spring and till the first of June,
1890, vigorously prosecuted.*

The opening of the basement and the dedication of the finished house, both occurring under
his pastorate, gave a promising opportunity to
Methodism in the city. The great and overflow-
ing congregations attending the first services were
indices of the public's appreciation of the new
place of worship. And with the comfort and other
agreeable features provided for worshipers, the
pews might and should have been kept filled on
the Lord's day. The mission of this central sanctuary is not fulfilled except it shall induce a house
full of attendants at the regular and ordinary Sabbath services.

Mr. Merrill had been in charge about nine
months when the basement was opened for use.
It accommodated half as many people as the auditorium into which the congregation was moved
nearly a year afterwards. The improved condition
gave encouragement to the patient but burdened
membership.

Revival services were held each winter without
resulting in the awakening of but few. The pastor
labored incessantly to promote a good work, but
not many ungodly were attracted to the house.
The services, however, were helpful in the sense
of enlivening those who took part.

---

* More particularly stated elsewhere.

Up to the date of the completion of the auditorium the pastor had too much outside work, causing the use of time that should have been spent in his study. As a consequence he fell below what was expected of him in the pulpit, and was never thereafter able to regain what was lost by such hindrance in the middle of his term.

In the pulpit Mr. Merrill was not able as demanded by the exigencies, though faithful in the discharge of all other duties of his office. In discoursing he was disposed to be elaborate and lengthy, two features that usually detract from a preacher's reputation, and invariably tend to tire instead of interesting an audience. In preparing his sermons he constructed them so as to include pertinent and theological points, which when presented would be instructive and pleasing, if condensed to an appropriate length.

After three years of service to this Church, at a time when too much was expected of him, he was transferred to the Pittsburgh Conference. During his stay the degree of D. D. was conferred upon him.

The First Methodist Episcopal Church having reached a date in its history when it was deemed needful that its pulpit should be filled by a preacher and pastor who could command respect on account of personal accomplishments of a high order. That such an one might be secured the officers of the Church began, in 1892, seeking, which effort resulted in the transfer of Rev. Frank Crane, and his appointment to this charge.

Mr. Crane belongs to the West, a native of Illinois, in which State he began life thirty-five years ago. He learned to correct false syntax and to investigate Greek radicals in the schools of his native State. He came from a large and influential Church at Bloomington to accept an Omaha pastorate, in which he has successfully served to the present.

His style in the pulpit is neither ornate nor diffuse. He makes choice of words that distinctly express his meaning without employing a superfluity of verbiage or waste of time in repetition: but keeps uppermost the line of thought suggested by his text or topic. He evidently prepares well for the pulpit, usually, and exhibits a personal interest in the theme of discourse. He makes, hence, the subject attractive, and gets the ears of listeners without much apparent effort. The sequel to this is, that he preaches to a well-filled house of deeply interested hearers.

Mr. Crane's appearance both in the pulpit and out of it, is that of a manly and sensible clergyman. He enjoys the company and fellowship of friends, and covets and gets the good opinion of many who are not communicants of his Church. He enjoys recreation as well as his books, and at the right time may be seen taking a little diversion astride of his bicycle. There are signs in his study that he reads the best of current literature, thus keeping up with the times in being familiar with writings and criticism on all questions of moment to mankind.

Pastor Crane lately introduced in his services what he pleases to term Pulpit editorials. Every Sunday evening he reads from manuscript one or more before taking his text. He treats in these brief essays national, political or municipal matters accordingly as the latest news or local occurrences may suggest. They are made up in a measure from the newspapers, and are intended for the better-enlightenment of young men who may not be able correctly to interpret passing events. This departure from prevailing custom has enough of the sensational to attract large congregations.

The Nebraska Wesleyan University, at the late commencement, June, 1895, conferred on Mr. Crane the degree of Doctor of Divinity.

CHAPTER IV.

CHURCH BUILDING IN SUBURBS.

NOT as in the country, the people of a city will not go far to attend religious services. If a place of worship of our own Church is not near at hand, many who have certificates of membership. and purpose making homes in town, are disposed to unite with some other denomination, the location of whose church is nearer their residences. This estrangement cannot be counteracted except by the erection of suburban edifices for the accommodation of such people. Sometimes, too, this leads to a weakening of a Society already organized. by making occasion for others to withdraw, which might have done better work if all had remained together.

The tendency of so many to make attendance at church personally easy, or, omit the going altogether, relapsing into indifference, has to be met, if possible. And the remedy is in the multiplication of places of worship. Omaha is not an exception to this law, as the subjoined sketches will show.

SUBURBAN CHURCHES.

The first movement towards forming a second Society in Omaha was of the date of August 14th, 1868, when the pastor of the First Church, Henry

C. Westwood, reports to his Quarterly conference the transfer of the following names to the Omaha Mission:

William Hunt,	Wyatt Kincade,
Walter G. Pigman,	S. Kincade,
Hester Pigman,	A. Stewart,
Simeon Pigman,	Nancy Stewart,
Chas. L. Pigman,	S. Spaulding,
Tho's J. Staley,	E. Wilbur,
S. Jennie Staley,	C. Tiffany,
P. A. Demorest,	A. Penny,
J. Crowel,	J. Adair.

The people of the northwest part of town, some of whom became restless under Mr. Westwood's administration, made that an occasion to ask for letters of dismissal. A few good people had begun a Sunday-school which was held in a rented building then standing on the east side of Twenty-third street, between Izard and Nicholas, and these transfers joined them in their endeavors to teach morals to the children. The attendance soon increased to nearly a hundred. Encouraged by this, no little deliberating ensued in respect to having a house of worship of their own.

The Mission flourished, and was frequently supplied with preaching. Every week added to the interest. The best advisers prevailed upon the membership, which was now equipped with everything but a house in which all comers might be accommodated, to proceed to the erection of a church building. The question was canvassed for more than a year, however, before an attempt was made, and even then it was a venture. Moses F. Shinn at that time owning an addition to the city north of the creek (now an underground storm sewer) that flowed through the town plat, cutting Twenty-first street, just east of Izard, made a proposition to donate a lot for a site. A majority of those in whose behalf the project was begun, was not pleased with the location. An offer was made by Zenas Stevens to exchange a lot valued at $800 lying at the southeast corner of Twenty-first and Izard streets for two of Mr. Shinn's lots, which offer was accepted, and the troublesome question of choosing a site was thus put at rest.

Mr. Shinn was interested in the enterprise, and, besides the two lots donated, voluntarily assisted by loaning $2,000 to the Trustees on condition such a building as he suggested might be erected. An effort was made to secure $2,500 more which was never all obtained: but a contract was let to Cyrus Rose and his brother Albert to construct a house, the size and features of which were on the plans, thirty by fifty-eight feet, costing $4,500. The edifice was two stories in height. The basement, entirely above ground, was intended as a Good Templars' hall, and the second floor as an auditorium.

Trustees were elected as follows: namely,

Zenas Stevens, L. H. Broadwell, Dr. M. G.
Anderson, John W. McCune and C. W. Cain.
The membership included, at the date of the
organization, June 11th, 1870, besides the Trustees,
such names as are here recorded: Mr. and Mrs.
E. A. Pickens, Mrs. Lizzie Staley, Mrs. J. W.
McCune, Mrs. L. H. Broadwell, Mr. and Mrs.
C. L. Bristol, Mrs. Clark Woodman, Mrs. P.
O'Hawes, James McKelvey, Mrs. John Shill, John
W. Tousley, W. G. Pigman, wife and sons, Mrs.
J. W. Dorsey, W. H. Woods, L. B. Whitmore,
R. M. Trout and wife, L. N. Freeman, Mrs. Allo-
way and A. Parmer.

The Second Church, as it was now known, was
dedicated June 26th, 1870, by Dr. J. W. Reid of
Chicago, at that time editor of the *Northwestern
Christian Advocate*. But the charge was left to
be supplied at the Conference in the spring, and
was without a preacher regularly to fill the pulpit.
Shortly after the dedication Geo. W. De La Matyr,
a transfer from Wisconsin, was appointed, and,
till the next spring served as pastor. The presiding elder, A. G. White, reports this charge as
having "overcome much opposition and grown
into considerable importance." In the statistics
forty members are reported, and a Sunday-school
with twelve teachers and one hundred and twenty-
five scholars.

Cyrus A. King, a transfer from the Maine Conference, was appointed in 1871, and faithfully did

the work of an evangelist. The same person, in his report to the Annual conference, says of Mr. King: "Bro. King makes religion a specialty in public and in private. He is a good preacher, an excellent pastor, and well adapted to cope with real life, intensified as it is in western customs and progress. There has been no special revival, but a revival influence has prevailed during most of the year and many have been converted and added to the Church."

Mr. King made a marked impression as an advocate of purity of heart and life; but he remained but one year, and was succeeded by C. McKelvey who had as much success as to be the means of awakening some revival interest. The salaries of both Mr. King and his immediate successor were liberally estimated, and, for the most part, paid.

This Society now began taking rank among the desirable appointments; and in prosperous times was able to support a popular minister in comfort. But at the date last named began feeling anxious about the debt remaining on the house. Efforts were made to collect old subscriptions, a large share of which had been obtained of members of the First Church, some of whom had not fully paid the sums promised. But the gathering of such remnants, as is usually the case, was difficult. The officers very keenly felt the annoyance, but were not able materially to change the aspect.

During these years the Society was largely
helped in the payment of current expenses by persons who themselves were not communicants,
whose wives were active in church affairs. Among
these willing contributors were Clark Woodman
and Pat. O'Hawes, names yet familiar to the
citizens of Omaha.

Joseph H. Presson, a young man of such gifts
as promised success, was appointed in the spring
of 1873 to take charge of the work. Except the
delinquency in getting rid of the encumbrance on
the property, Mr. Presson had a prosperous year
which was extended to eighteen months by the
change in the time of the meeting of the Annual
conference from April to October. During this
year a new feature presented itself unexpectedly to
the private membership. A proposal was made by
the several members who had withdrawn from the
First Church on account of the irritation produced
by a refusal of the Quarterly conference to approve
Samuel Burns as superintendent of the Sunday-
school. looking to the purchasing of the house.
The pastor was favorable to disposing of the
building, and an agreement was made, without
submitting the case to the Annual conference, con-
ditional upon Mr. Shinn's releasing the purchasers
from any obligations to him. Mr. Shinn held a
mortgage on the house, and made the demand
that the sum he used in aiding its erection should
be refunded. But a compromise was effected by

the purchasers paying him one half the sum he expended.

The purpose of the removal of the building was the principal object of the buyers, Messrs. Burns, Homan and Steele, as principals. At once a square of ground lying at the southeast corner of Eighteenth and California streets, extending south to the alley, was bought of A. J. Poppleton at a cost of $2,500, and the moving of the church was undertaken. Mr. Burns managed the drawing of the church from the original site to the new one, and energetically pushed the work of making the house ready for occupation. The cost of repairing and furnishing added to the expense of hauling was $2,500, which sum was soon after provided for at the dedication.

The dimensions of the building were after removal the same as before, as no change was made in its size or external appearance. But the basement was partitioned so as to make three class rooms and a kitchen. Two of the rooms were separated by folding doors and could easily be thrown together to accommodate a prayer meeting or sociable. The veteran itinerant, Dr. Thomas B. Lemon, was besought to accept the pastorate, and at the Conference the same fall was appointed. The new place of worship was dedicated November 2d, 1874, by Professor (now Bishop) W. X. Ninde, of Evanston, Illinois, assisted by Dr. Lemon, J. H. Presson and Rev. Reuben Gaylord of the

Congregational church. It was henceforth named the Eighteenth Street church. Dr. Lemon organized his working force by nominating as Trustees G. W. Homan, R. C. Steele. Samuel Burns, L. B. Whitmore, C. L. Garrison, Zenas Stevens and J. Palmer, some of whom were also elected Stewards.

Mr. Lemon labored to increase the efficiency of the Church, and was the means of winning friends, as well as souls to Christ, among them some who are yet honoring the Master. The year, however, was not fruitful of results as he desired, and his measure of usefulness was not satisfactory to himself, though he commanded the respect of old and new acquaintances. At the ending of the year he returned to the Nebraska City District whence he came to accept this charge at the instance of some Omaha friends, among whom he had lived long before when serving as pastor of the First Church and as presiding elder of the district including this city. His support in salary was ample as he received for the year's services $1,300, and never forgot the days he spent at Eighteenth Street church.

The next year I. N. Pardee succeeded to the charge. He was a new man, well educated and a good preacher. During his term of two years, particularly in the latter winter, an awakening of some import was enjoyed. Altogether, taking into account the building of a parsonage, he was instru-

mental in doing a praiseworthy work. His salary
the second year was $1,400 and paid, and a large
Sunday-school was kept in effective order. The
number in full membership in the Church was one
hundred and thirty.

REV. P. C. JOHNSON.

In the fall of 1877, P. C. Johnson, on Dr.
Lemon's recommendation, was appointed, and
served under a shadow for one year. He was an
efficient man; but the hard times opposed his

utmost efforts to accomplish as much as he was
capable of doing with a fair chance. The Church
manifested too much indifference to allow of his
being encouraged, but the rather wrought in him a
feeling akin to helplessness. Mr. Johnson was a
man of such sensitiveness as to feel very keenly
the shake of a left hand, but there was no course
left him to pursue except to make the best of
a misfit. His conduct was creditable to himself, and $1,200 was paid as a salary; and his
next appointment removed him to South Tenth
Street. .

W. K. Beans, late of the Rock River Conference, Illinois, now, 1878. became pastor at Eighteenth street. His accomplishments soon gained
for him a reputation as a man above the ordinary.
In the pulpit he carried himself gracefully, exhibit-
ing as much self-confidence as to assure the hearers
that he is prepared to make a deliverance that
would be helpful. His heavy voice, well trained,
is in his favor, though it is by no means musical
when used in speech. He is a careful thinker, and
his thoughts are uttered under accurate discipline
in the delivery of a sermon. Points are stated and
argued while he holds well to the subject of discourse. Making no pretension to brilliancy, he
nevertheless usually keeps the attention of listeners to the close, and his sermons are not wearisome
on account of length—a virtue to be adhered to by
men of less note.

Mr. Beans' acceptibility led to his continuance for three years; and this period was a season of the Church's greatest prosperity. Every interest of the charge was cared for by the pastor, and in turn, he was well sustained by the membership.

REV. WESLEY K. BEANS.

The pastorate was next given, by appointment, to J. W. Shank, the present editor-in-chief of the *Omaha Christian Advocate*, who was commended by his past experience and work. Of industrious habits, he took hold of the work with the purpose of making himself felt in the administration of clerical and pastoral duty. His beginning was in 1881, and finding the roster and plans of operating as left by his predecessor in good shape, his commencing was the easier. For two years he persistently kept astir in an endeavor to maintain the character of the Church; and if he could have had only the people to care for his term might have been most agreeable: but a debt on the property that had been standing too long gave him and his brethren a good deal of concern. The officers were debating as to the best means of procedure—whether it might not be in the interests of the Church and serve the cause of religion to sell their property, cancel their mortgage, and invest the balance in a new location. Mr. Shank favored the latter opinion, and made an attempt to unite the First Church and the one he was serving in building a great central structure that would accommodate both. Failing in this, he began negotiations the latter year of his term with the object of acquiring a new site at the corner of Clark and Nineteenth streets, even proceeding so far as to accept subscriptions from Messrs. Kountze and Poppleton with a view of exchanging the real estate and buildings belonging to the Church for the site above named. This proposal did not meet with sufficient favor to be carried into execution; and the plan was frustrated on the near approach

of the session of the Conference, and at the session
the pending negotiations were made void.   This is
accounted for on the score of Mr. Shank's anxiety
to give all the assistance he could in helping the

REV. JOHN W. SHANK, D. D.

Society out of debt, and at the same time commence making provision for a new site for a
church.   The restlessness of the people whom he
served suggested the making haste to provide also

a new house. Another pastor was appointed to follow Mr. Shank in the person of J. B. Leedom.

The struggle under the new administration continued, giving the new pastor great anxiety as to what might be the outcome. He seemed for a while to be confused and was not able to grasp the trend of affairs. And when eventually brought face to face with the situation, felt that it were next to useless to try to perpetuate the name of Eighteenth Street Church. Before the close of the winter, however, a protracted meeting was held jointly with the First Church, Chas. W. Savidge being at that date pastor of the latter. The services were alternated, but the former had in a measure lost its hold upon the public, and Mr. Leedom was unable, though using all of his ability, to attract the attendance of many people. Hence the extraordinary service brought about no helpful result.

More than ever the trustees were now inclined to dispose of their property, and on July 11th, 1884, sold the lot on which the parsonage stood, including the house; and on September 24th following made sale of the church building and lot. A lot also on the immediate corner of California and Eighteenth streets was disposed of, netting, with the others, the sum of $10,500. A condition of sale was that possession should be given at once. Therefore Mr. Leedom vacated the preacher's house and moved to Seward street.

The Swedish Methodists bought the church house and desired its occupancy. Suspending services in English, Mr. Leedom had no place to which he could invite people to worship. But the mortgage of $3,000 on the property was cancelled, and the Society was relieved of indebtedness. Thus ends the history of a project that was undertaken not with the best of motives, and the caprice was frustrated by the closing of all avenues to success!

SEWARD STREET CHURCH.

The Society so recently left without property, though discomfited for the time being, was not disposed to disband. Having now $7,500 to invest in a new site and house of worship, a lot was selected and purchased at the north-east corner of Twenty-second and Seward streets, at a cost of $1,500. The deed was made by Dr. C. L. Hart and wife to the Trustees, J. M. Marston, Joseph B. West, Edward B. Wood, George J. Hadden and Zenas Stevens, at that date constituting the Board. Pastor Leedom personally decided upon plans for a brick structure, and immediately began arranging to put in a foundation.

But the Conference year closed soon afterwards, and R. L. Marsh was appointed the first pastor of Seward Street Church. During the ensuing four months the membership worshiped for a few Sabbaths in the vacant store building belonging to Charles Bruner, at the north-west corner of Hamilton and Twenty-fourth streets. From this place a removal was made to the basement of the Presbyterian church on Twenty-fourth street near Nicholas.

A contract was let for the brick work of the new house to B. F. Baker, and the carpenter work to John Henry. The underground walls were laid, which, when of a height such as to receive the corner stone, a service was held at the site, October 14th, 1884, on which occasion Dr. J. B. Maxfield, presiding elder, officiated. The stone was laid, subscriptions asked for and obtained, and all were pleased with the prospect. Mr. Marsh, endorsed by the Trustees, untiringly persisted in soliciting subscriptions, promises and money during the following winter and spring, and was successful in this as in everything in his line of duty. The structure now begun was thirty-four by fifty-four feet in dimensions on the ground, built from the Church Extension Society's plans. The work was rapidly prosecuted, and soon as the walls were reared and the roof put on and the floor laid the Society began using it for services, and on the 20th of January, 1885, the house was for the first time occupied. And on the 10th of May, Rev. R. N. McKaig, of Lincoln, dedicated the church to the worship of God. The building and lot cost $7,500, and with a loan of $2,500 the members were enabled nearly to free themselves from debt, including the furnishing of the auditorium.

Henceforth this Society took on new life, and with commendable zeal and interest made efforts to become an aggressive Church. The harmony prevailing was indicative of the end sought—the reformation of surrounding neighborhoods. Mr. Marsh now had the privilege of preaching in the completest and best Methodist church building in the city, and with equal diligence gave heed to legitimate pastoral duties. The Society also accomplished much more in its own behalf than ever before in permanently building up, and was happy in the use and possession of its new home.

Mr. Marsh, as was his purpose at the first, served but one year, and temporarily quit the pastorate that he might attend college and fit himself better for the ministry. He was superceded by C. W. Savidge, in 1885, who, flushed with uninterrupted success at the First Church, popularly entered upon the performance of his obligations to God and the people whom he was called upon to serve. In preaching, praying and carefully visiting his flock, he soon became acquainted with their religious life at their homes. Particularly gave he heed to the young people and sought to lead them to Christ. His congregation grew larger and was respectfully attentive. The second year in charge he repeatedly preached sensational sermons which attracted more people than the house would accommodate, and the Trustees soon began maturing plans to add to its capacity, resulting in the erection of an annex which increased the superficial floor space to twice the area of the original. The cost of the addition, including furnace and furniture, was $9,577.

Mr. Savidge remained three years, and, in the meantime, was married to a lady of literary acquirements who was the means of assisting him in his work. He also published a small book entitled "Shots from my Pulpit," containing a number of his best sermons.

W. M. Worley followed Mr. Savidge to the pastorate of this Church in the fall of 1888. His demeanor both in public and also in the homes of his people was so unlike his predecessor that he with some timidity encountered the nonchalance of his membership. He was not inclined to adopt in the pulpit any methods other than the most regular order of services, and his preaching was after the style of older men and without embellishment—steady, practical and biblical. His faithfulness in the performance of his ministerial duties was, as he judged, right, and usually would have been approved as correct. But he was not free from criticism on account of a little lack of city polish—he had never spent time in studying parlor etiquette. Before the ending of the year he decided there are places better adapted to his gifts and graces than Seward Street Church. The number of members had now reached nearly three hundred and fifty, and a liberal salary was paid the pastor, as well as good support was given the Sunday-school in providing requisites.

In 1889 H. A. Crane succeeded Mr. Worley, and served till 1892, making a creditable record as pastor and preacher. Well educated, studious, and possessing good social qualities, he secured the esteem of his people, and was useful to an extent further than merely building up, but in promoting cordiality in the Church and cementing fraternity. The opinion prevails that he and his people were mutually well pleased.

Before the close of his term deciding that, in order to satisfy his convictions, he must be obedient to a call to go to a foreign missionary field, soon after Conference he prepared for his departure to Bombay, India, under control of the parent Missionary society.

Dr. D. K. Tindall was appointed September, 1892, to this now promising charge, and with his versatile gifts opened up lines of work the most sure to result in the greatest good. He was most favorably received and given all the opportunity he could expect to promote the cause of righteousness. In the pulpit, the Sunday-school and the young people's organization he was efficient and kindly welcome. The officers of the Church responded to his requests for help, and soon all the machinery was set in motion. Expectation was rife, and the pastor was eager to witness developments. He stood at the helm during his incumbency directing

every movement of the Church, and his was such
success as comes of working in the interests of the
people.

Mr. Tindall's masculine voice and his ability in

REV. DANIEL K. TINDALL, D. D.

song-singing enlivened his pulpit performances as
well as the prayer and class meetings. His choice
of subjects and his skill in handling them in the
pulpit gave zest to the services. He spent two

years successfully in the charge, and would have
been returned, but, he was thought to be needed
by the authorities, more elsewhere.

W. K. Beans, having served Trinity Church
for five years. was removed to Seward Street,
October, 1894. He had held a pastoral office
in the city eight years and was, hence, widely
known by the population only to be respected
for his ability in the pulpit and as a gentleman in
social circles. He had been a witness, in this
long service in the city, of the great strides Methodism made, as every opportunity was used to
build up the denomination. His associates in
the pulpits of the other charges co-operated in
bringing to pass a continual growth. Together,
then, they deserve the praise.

SOUTH TENTH STREET CHURCH.

In the spring of 1872, the city in the meantime
having spread out southward and beyond the
Union Pacific railway crossing on Tenth street,
making the distance too great for the old Church
to attract people, a mission was formed, with
Joseph M. Adair in charge. First Church as it
was then and has since been known was located on
Seventeenth street, between Dodge and Capitol
avenue. This new field included not only the
south end of town, but some points outside were
attached forming a circuit. Mr. Adair mentions
in his diary Omaha, Florence, Papillion, Iron

Bluffs, Richards', Bird's school-house and Pickens's as places where preaching was held.

It appears that the missionary sought out by traversing the territory the places named, except the villages, and carried the gospel to neighborhoods between the towns. His dependence for food and raiment for himself and family was upon a few and scattered church members and friends who were engaged in making homes for themselves. His receipts were discouragingly small, which would have led a less courageous itinerant to quitting the work. This meager support, however, was partly relieved by presents of small quantities of articles such as his family was in need of, and they managed to live without suffering but little from want.

There was not a church building in his field when he assumed charge of the work except at Florence: and the places for holding services were primitive, and in the winter season, uncomfortable. He endured all these privations without complaint, deeming it a great privilege to have authority to present the cross of Christ to gainsaying and rebellious people, seldom alluding to the matter of scanty subsistence.

During the second and third years of his term of service he fared better, and was signally useful and happy in his office. The last year, 1874, he raised a large sum to apply on paying the debt on the church and lot in Omaha which was purchased in the first year of his pastorate. The building was small but served as a place in which to preach and conduct a Sunday-school. From this earnest planning and executing there have resulted many pleasant reminiscences.

About the time of the autumnal equinox, in 1875, the eccentric and volatile T. H. Tibbles was given charge of the little church in which worshiped a small membership of poor people. The other appointments were adjusted to other charges or abandoned, among the latter, Florence. Before the close of the next spring, Mr. Tibbles secured a promise from Bishop Andrews, whose episcopal home at that date was at Des Moines, Iowa, to come to Omaha, and dedicate the house. The B shop came and preached, but refused to utter the dedicatory formula, saying the people should build better before giving a house to God's service.

Mr. Tibbles was a stenographer and newspaper reporter, and rather than depend upon the membership to provide a salary, he gave more time to writing for which he was in a small way compensated. The charge, hence, did not prosper in his care, but he added to its indebtedness by having a parsonage built on the south side of the meeting house at a cost of about $800, most of which was provided for, but the remnant was added and put down as debt, and the property was mortgaged to secure it.

The following two years the church was left to

be supplied, and the opinion obtained that such a charge was not deserving of the services of a preacher, and probably would have been omitted from the list of appointments except for counsel to the contrary by John P. Roe, a supernumerary of Wisconsin Conference, who had located in the south part of town. The presiding elder placed the work in Mr. Roe's control, and the latter made a proposition to the membership that his taking charge would be on condition of their paying one-fourth of the indebtedness on the property every quarter, which they agreed to do. Another proposition made by him was that if they succeeded in cancelling a due proportion of the debt they should have his services gratis the first three months, and continuously for a year, in case a certificate of deposit for twenty-five per cent. of their debt should be exhibited at each meeting of the Quarterly conference. The total was met, and all legal embarrassment removed from their property in twelve months.

The success of the first year with Mr. Roe as their minister and adviser led to their desiring a continuance of his services and ministry which had been so valuable the former year. The presiding elder reappointed him; and the officers of the Church were called upon to meet their pastor before the year's work was planned. He proposed if they would guarantee a salary of $500 that, on the receipt of the sum, it would be laid

aside to be used in aid of a new building enterprise
which was in contemplation but not yet projected.
The conditions on the part of both were complied
with, and the sequel is to be found in the story
at a later date.

P. C. Johnson, who had been stationed at
Eighteenth street in this city, in 1878 was appointed
to this charge. Keenly feeling the humiliation of
being obliged to make such a sacrifice he was not
in a state of mind fitting him to enjoy his new
surroundings. Though a pulpit man possessing
more than a smattering of theological lore and
gifts in preaching entitling him to expect a better
place, he remained with these people worshiping
and officiating in a small and uninviting house to
the end of the year. Without ambition to try to
do much, very little was wrought for the better-
ment of the charge; not even was any promising
attempt made to provide a more commodious
house. The question, however, was often broached,
and particularly the need was canvassed frequently,
but no decision to make an effort was reached,
much to the discomfiture of interested parties.
That part of town was building up, and hence the
population increasing, making the necessity for
improved accommodations for worship more and
more apparent; but the courage of the Church was
not of such measure as to lead to any decisive
attempt, though the $500 of Mr. Roe's bequest
was held in reserve for such purpose.

David Marquette, an earnest pastor and tireless worker, was appointed by Bishop Harris to this yet feeble but determined charge in the fall of 1879, and enjoyed a term of unqualified success.

REV. DAVID MARQUETTE.

He had not much more than entered upon his pastoral work till he began gathering subscriptions to purchase a lot upon which to erect a new church and parsonage. His efforts were so encouraging to himself and his brethren that a site was selected and the ground purchased at the south-west corner of Tenth and Pierce streets, at a cost of $1,200. After a respite of twelve months and the sale of the old property was consummated, Mr. Marquette proceeded to accomplish the building of a new house of worship. He was the instance also of the erection of a two-story preacher's house.

To carry out his plans the persistent preacher with unflagging interest kept up the canvass for money till he had gone over the best part of the city, applying personally to men in the railway, express and business offices. He obtained a large number of small sums, and enough to risk the finishing of the building ready for occupation. As is usually the case, however, as much more was required as to make necessary an urgent call for cash at the dedication.

The patrons of the enterprise had contributed to the extent of their ability; the sale of the old sanctuary and parsonage and the real estate, additional to the reserve fund from Mr. Roe's administration, enabled the sanguine preacher and his people to meet a large share of the expenses incurred, and mutually rejoiced at seeing their long contemplated hopes realized. The membership was increased to double the number he found on taking charge.

The completion of the house was effected in the third year of Mr. Marquette's pastorate, and on the

tenth of July, 1881, was formally dedicated by
Bishop John F. Hurst.

Henceforward this field was increasingly desirable. and in the fall of 1882, J. W. Stewart was
transferred from the First Church of this city to
take charge of South Tenth Street. Immediately
the attendants felt the impression of his practical
and searching discourses. Mr. Stewart's labors
deserved appreciation as he made himself useful
in the homes of his people, and in the prayer and
revival meetings as well as in the pulpit. He was
loyally a Methodist, and no unfavorable criticism
could be made on his orthodoxy. Nothing
afforded him more pleasure than the legitimate
work of the ministry. In this charge his family
enjoyed the use of a new and comfortable parsonage, and the people provided an ample support by
a good salary. The uplift given the Society in
possessing a new church and other paraphernalia
necessary to attracting the people, was much in
the pastor's favor, hence, he had the advantage of
any of his predecessors.

Mr. Stewart remained two years, and was then
transferred to the Nebraska Conference, where he
has labored unremittingly till the present, regarded
by his co-workers as a trusty and successful
pastor.

E. G. Fowler came next in succession to the
pastorate of this charge in 1884, and without mis-
givings entered upon his official duties, amid the

dubiousness of his people as to his physical ability. His slight body and delicate appearance did not prepossess many in his favor; but his original and intellectual efforts in testimony meetings and in sermonizing soon won for him the good will of a great share of his parishioners. He was put at a disadvantage, too, in having to struggle with constitutional infirmities, and while desirous of performing full services, his precarious health forbade his effecting all he coveted to be able to do. His integrity and devotion as well as his mental ability made of him a good friend and adviser in trouble, and a safe counselor in matters of conscience.

The Society during his stay of two years was kept in good trim, and, in return, paid him a good salary. Though the membership hardly exceeded one hundred, he reported liberal collections for all the benevolences, without a blank! This feature of the case is in proof of his efficiency, and that nothing was purposely neglected that would in any way contribute to the reputation of the charge.

T. C. Clendening, not long since from Illinois, succeeded Mr. Fowler, and found the affairs of the charge in such condition as to permit of his taking hold where his predecessor left off; and he quickly made himself acquainted with the religious habits of his membership.

If hard work and enthusiasm are of account in an itinerant's life and work, Mr. Clendening has a claim of being difficult to excel. His services were prized on account of his alertness in caring for every interest of the Church. In the pulpit he was clear, argumentative and convincing. His

REV. T. C. CLENDENING, D.D.

sermons were well studied, written and arranged; and, bating a fault in vocalization, were delivered so as to attract the hearing and reach the hearts of his auditors.

During the second year of his pastorate of this Church, and on the removal, in 1887, of Rev. J. W. Phelps to California, vacating the Omaha District, Mr. Clendening was chosen to assume the office of presiding elder, the duties of which calling he performed till September, 1893. No less so than in the pastorate, his labors were fruitful of results. He was resolute and willing to share in the hard work with his preachers, never attempting to excuse himself from being present where most needed. At the close of a term of five and a half years on the District, he was appointed to Wesley Church, Walnut Hill, a populous suburb of Omaha. After serving this Church a few months, he was sought for as a field agent of the Nebraska Wesleyan University, at Lincoln, in which position he still serves with acceptability.

This charge had now reached a condition of importance so great that any neglect in caring for its interests would be damaging. Therefore, the authorities began seeking a capable man to follow Mr. Clendening. C. N. Dawson, in the second year of his term at North Bend, was invited and consented to remove to Omaha, and arrived April 1st, 1887. He was soon domiciled in the parsonage at South Tenth street, and heartily set about operating in behalf of the Church. The membership very cordially joined with him in an endeavor to widen the influence of the Society. He was of such age as to have had experience, and yet youthful enough to be buoyant and ambitious to excel.

Mr. Dawson was reappointed twice, serving till the autumn of 1890. At each year's beginning and throughout his term, he with apparently renewed vigilance kept an eye on every opportunity to make himself useful. And with his gifts in preaching and singing as well as his easy facility of adapting himself to the Sunday-school, soon made him a favorite of the young people. These qualities added to his cheerful and unaffected kindness endeared him to his brethren, and made easier his access to their hearts.

The term of his service was mixed with pleasure, and his usefulness and name are yet in the memory of the people. It is almost needless to say that his labors effected great good for the Society and neighborhood. He is now serving the fifth year at the First Church, South Omaha, where, during the term, the house of worship having burned, he had the management of the erection of a new and better one in which his people now worship.

Alfred Hodgetts, having just closed a term on the Elkhorn Valley district, followed Mr. Dawson as preacher-in-charge, in the autumn of 1890, and found the Society in good spirits waiting to receive him and his family. His cordial habits and ease in entertaining were equal to those of his predecessor, enabling him to secure and hold the friendship of numerous people. The sacred desk was

no more his forte than the amiability of his
demeanor.

Mr. Hodgetts' robust health was in his favor,
permitting him to labor without fatigue. Confine-
ment to his study and books was apparently no

REV. ALFRED HODGETTS, D. D.

detriment to his physical strength. But he enjoyed
and used the open air in calls upon the membership, and in these visits laid hold of whatever
would contribute to illustrate from the pulpit reli-

gious life and prospects of those to whom he
preached. His sermons, hence, were not merely
theological, but practical as well, and stimulating
to his hearers. He enjoys pastoral work because
it brings him in close contact with the people
whom he serves. His record at South Tenth
Street was to him and his people, in the main, satisfactory.

During this term of service the degree of Doctor of Divinity was conferred upon him, which he
bore with seeming pleasure.

T. C. Webster, late of Walnut Hill, was designated to take charge of this station in 1893. His
thorough and successful work heretofore was an
indication of what might be expected of him. His
methods were soon made known, and there was a
very general acquiescence in his plans. Dr. Maxfield, his presiding elder, reports of this charge in
these words: "South Tenth Street has come
through this hard year with credit to itself and
honor to its pastor.   *   *   *   It has had good
revival work this year."

Mr. Webster wrought earnestly with the purpose of being helpful. He was not a novitiate.
but a man of practice in the pulpit and in all the
work of the pastoral office. Such advice as he
gave as well as his instructions were mature and
scriptural. His sermons were full of meat on
which the soul might fatten. Never thoughtless,
nor indifferent to the weal of the Church, but seek-

ing to be used of God as an instrument for doing
good. His devotion and ability were of such
measure as to qualify him for successful service.

He is always disposed to deal gently with his

REV. T. C. WEBSTER.

membership, preferring to accomplish correction
without arraigning any before a committe for the
purpose of investigating complaints. As a counselor he is candid, firm and decisive, nearly certain

of winning the one whom he is disciplining to accepting his terms. But he makes no unreasonable requirements, yet he holds any who are disposed to be insubordinate to the scriptural law in respect to behavior.

Mr. Webster's discretion in administering discipline commends him at once to those who must be visited for the purpose of exhorting or persuading to a more correct religious life. Himself first setting a good example of a practical walk and circumspect piety, he the more easily can commend such demeanor.

The membership had now reached nearly two hundred, and were able to pay their pastor a salary on which he could live respectably.

J. B. Priest, a comparatively young man with a good record, was appointed in October, 1894, to this Church, and already is able to report progress. Mr. Priest is making an effort to comprehend the reason for the less success of that Church compared with some others which have been organized in later years, and thinks he will be able to explain the cause when he completes his investigations. Probably the location might be better; and, may be, some other causes have contributed to its want of the greatest efficiency. If his suggestions and plans shall meet with favor, he will work out a demonstration of the possibilities of the Church.

The membership is ready to second any move-

ment that promises a successful ending, but are
not disposed to barter their property, now so
valuable, without full compensation.   They are
unwilling to be left without a place to hold services
till provision is made to change this location for a
better one.   The Official Board is composed of

REV. JAMES B. PRIEST.

those who are on the lookout for nothing but that
which is practicable, and refuse to adopt any expedients that do not promise not only holding the
Society together, but the bettering its condition
and prospects.

They and the pastor are in agreement as to the

wisest course to pursue, and are only waiting for
the time and opportunity to favor their preferences,
when unitedly they will make a movement. Or,
if thought best, will remain on the present site till
it becomes more valuable, or business begins
crowding too close upon their premises now held
and occupied as a place of worship.

CHAPTER V.

THE Methodist Episcopal Church since its organization has favored the teaching of the Bible to the children and youth. The preachers at the beginning and for a long time gave time and attention to catechising the children at their homes. Confidence in the inspired Word and its verity led the pastors and people to co-operate in giving the young a training in the fundamental doctrines and faith of the Church. This method of instruction was, after a while, in a measure neglected, and still more so in recent years has gone into disuse. The Sunday-school as now managed is a substitute by agreement of parties who should be most interested; which is equivalent to turning over the childhood of the Church to be instructed by persons not immediately concerned for their religious welfare.

The results of such training became so apparent that wise men discerning the need of doing something to counteract the cause, and effect a partial reform, organized the Epworth League. The young people of families of our denomination were inclined to leave the Sunday-school at the very age when most exposed to danger and needing most the restraints of Christian guardianship.

The homiletical and superficial method of teaching generalities to some of the scholars is not to the liking of many who have reached such years as to begin reading and thinking for themselves. Even the most accomplished and devoted teachers of Bible classes fail to interest such as are inclined to waywardness. But a large number, if at all serious, crave to be acquiring facts and doctrines relating to a positively religious life, and those of our own households want to be taught in regard to the law and government of the Church—the book of DISCIPLINE.

The time had come, too, when our own youth on account of neglect to instruct them in Methodism, knew no difference between the doctrines and government of the Church in which they had been reared and those of any other sect or denominational organization. Never having been made acquainted with the distinctive features of Methodism, they acquired no admiration of it. Under this regimen the Church was losing, and likely to fail of keeping its own young people; hence provision was made furnishing both instruction and work in the League, Senior and Junior, that our offspring might be educated in all the peculiarities of Methodism, and become intelligent and devoted members of the Church.

But the Sunday-school cannot be dispensed with, as the younger children need the tutoring it provides; and very soon the League will yield teachers with capabilities to impart instruction of another order than that which has obtained quite long enough.

This chapter is given to the treatment of the Sunday-school of the First Methodist Episcopal Church as far as the records furnish data, and the history of the schools of other charges is noted in their appropriate places.

Mrs. Geo. A. McCoy, who is still living and a resident of Omaha, now, and for a long time, a widow, was the instance of organizing the first Methodist Sunday-school. The beginning was on July 13th, 1856, and at the house then known as the Byers' property, on the south-west corner of Tenth and Farnam streets, at that date occupied by herself and husband. Fifteen children were summoned together. Gov. Izard was present, and responded to a call to make some remarks to the pupils on the occasion. It is related that there was no one present to lead in prayer, but a man of the name of Virtue repeated the Lord's prayer.

In December of the same year the school was removed to the new church on Thirteenth street, and Wm. R. Demorest was chosen superintendent. The teachers were William Ripley, Mrs. McCoy, Mrs. Bryant, and Mrs. Geo. W. Homan. This corps of instructors would signify that there was an increasing attendance. The first Library was presented by Moses F. Shinn, who was in those days actively engaged in church work. It is due that Mrs.

McCoy should have credit for preserving the outline facts of the above paragraphs of history relating to the origin of the Sunday-school in Omaha City.

In the fall of 1857, John W. Tousley, who had a few months before united with the Church by letter, was elected superintendent of the school, and held the office for nine years. In the meantime efforts were made to increase the attendance and interest. The facilities for instruction at that time in use were neither as accessible nor numerous as at the present. Teachers commonly provided themselves with question books and Longking's Notes, which, though the best helps, were far below the standards in use now. The superintendent was depended upon to give life to the school, and had to resort to all kinds of justifiable expedients to keep up an interest.

Pastor Slaughter succeeded Mr. Tousley, in 1866, as superintendent, and infused by his superior knowledge and tact a good degree of interest into the school. He reports before the expiration of his term that there are three Sunday-schools, and the prospects in each flattering. One of these was a Mission school in the north part of town, and another among the colored people. Mr. Slaughter's pastorate and superintendency closed at the same time, after more than two years of successful service.

In the statistics for 1866 only two schools are reported, giving the items below:

No. of officers and teachers............... 25
No. of scholars........................... 225
No. of infant scholars 40
No. of volumes in library.............. 350
Expenses of school......................$300

Mr. J. W. Tousley was again elected superintendent, but not without a contest. C. L. Garrison was a popular and capable Sunday-school worker, whose friends put him forward as a candidate, and the votes were nearly evenly divided.

The statistics for the next year vary but little from the last quoted; and for the year 1868 a falling off is shown resulting from the withdrawal of some whose help had previously been of avail to the school.

In 1869, after the Society enjoyed the occupancy of the new church on Seventeenth street, Samuel Burns was elected to the chief office of the School and served till 1874. The School under his regimen took on new life, becoming more and more popular and efficient, as shown by the succeeding report made by the Secretary to the Quarterly conference, June 5th, 1870:

No. of officers and teachers 37
No of scholars, including Bible class.. 286
Highest number attending any session. 336
Volumes in library.................. 533
Receipts of money for the year........$1,294.14
Total sum expended 1,208.90

The growth of the School and the equipments are made apparent even the more so from the report of the Presiding Elder, A. G. White, to the Annual conference. He says: "The Sunday-school (March, 1871) now numbers nearly four hundred. The best available talent is engaged, and money without stint is judiciously applied to make the School a model in all its appointments."

At a meeting of the Quarterly conference, February 9th, 1872, the report respecting the School is still more flattering, and reads thus:

No. of officers and teachers.............. .. 35
Total number of scholars enrolled 667
No. under fifteen years, except infant class ...410
No. of scholars in infant class 142
Expenses this year $1,154.50
No. of Sunday-school Advocates taken.......200
No. of Sunday-school Journals taken 30
No. of conversions of scholars.............. 30

Mr. Burns acted upon the score of Dr. Vincent's saying that three g's are essential in running a Sunday-school—grace, gumption and greenbacks.

Presiding Elder White, in reporting his District at the meeting of the Conference, March, 1872, has this to say of the school of the First Church: "The Sunday-school seems each session to be at the very zenith of excellence. The officers and teachers present a rare example of promptness and adaptability. Whatever money can purchase and judicious management and faithful labor accomplish are applied to make Sunday-school instruction attractive and successful."

Mr. Burns seemed not at all aware of the danger of standing on this giddy height of splendid success, and may have been imprudent in maintaining that he should be allowed the exclusive control of the Sunday-school irrespective of any other parties. and that no one else had any such claim as to expect to be taken into partnership or counsel in its management, or in any way interfere with his plans. The disposition arbitrarily to adhere to such a policy brought opposition, which resulted in his defeat. But it is the part of a faithful historian to state that the Sunday-school of this Church has never since reached the point of excellence to which it had attained under his supervision.

Of a session of the Quarterly conference, June 27th, 1874, the following minute is recorded: "On motion, the Conference voted by ballot on the approval of Samuel Burns as superintendent of Sunday-school, resulting in three for and ten against his approval." A controversy, hurtful to the Church and school, grew out of this movement, materially effecting both parties, alienating former friends and co-workers, and was made the occasion of the withdrawal of Mr. Burns and his coadjutors, who, on their own motion re-elected him superintendent. This dissolution at once resulted in their establishing another school, and, soon after, another Church.

M. G. McKoon was elected superintendent,

but the School's efficiency was impaired to the extent, by what had preceded, that no one's personal popularity was sufficient to counteract the effect.

Succeeding Mr. McKoon, J. Phipps Roe was elected in 1876, but, for some reason, holding the office only a short time, was succeeded, under Dr. Fisher's administration, by J. L. Webster, in 1877. Mr. Webster entered upon the discharge of his duties with enthusiasm, and possessing the qualities of a successful head of the School, kept the attendance respectably numerous, though including scarcely any pupils more than of the families of the Church. The new church building then in contemplation making the demand on the membership of all the money they could spare, the School had to be carried on with the using of very meagre cash support.

Under date of September 17th, 1877, the pastor reported as to the school:

> Average attendance, June, 250.
> Average attendance, July, 237.
> Average attendance, August, 220.
> Average for the quarter, 236.
> Cash collected, $138.97.

At a session of the Quarterly conference, May 7th, 1878, the report signified a larger average attendance—260.

The later history of the Sunday-schools of our Churches is so intimately connected with the work of the Societies, and so often mentioned, that it is needless to preserve a continuous record further.

Indeed, the records of the First Church for a few years are not accurate enough to serve the purpose of the historian. Omissions and other faults are to be found, rendering them unreliable when facts and other data are sought for. The task of gathering and formulating this history of the Sunday-school is so great that it consumed time that could be more advantageously employed.

There are a few observations that should be made, however, respecting the successful handling of the Sunday-school of the mother church at the present. Mr. Frank W. Hills is Superintendent, and is aided by the pastor and a large number of well-drilled teachers. The chief Bible class and the infant school are great features of the organization. And the largest attendance for several years now meets at noon every Sunday.

METHODISM IN SUBURBS.

CHAPTER VI.

THE continual growth of the city, and the selection of lots on which to build residences further from the center, made occasion for the erection of churches in the suburbs. Since 1882, the spreading of the town to the south-west, and the laying out of the high, undulating land from which many pieces were soon sold to seekers of locations for permanent homes, forcasted that which is seen to-day in the vicinity of Hanscom Park. In a few years the population had increased till churches had to be provided, as well as schools for the children.

As early as the spring of 1886, John Dale, wife, and five sons, yet holding membership in the First Church, removed to this inviting location now coming into prominence as a quiet, homelike community. There was no place of worship of their own denomination easier of access than that from which they had just removed. They were not satisfied; and Mr. Dale and his wife began an inspection of the neighborhood for the purpose of finding others of their faith, and were rewarded by being able to count twenty-two, including their own household, namely, John Dale, Ellen Dale, J. F. Dale, W. E. Dale, A. B. Dale, W. H. Dale, L. R. Dale, F. B. Dale, John L. Wilkie, Mrs. L. Wilkie, Mrs. Hamilton, Mrs. E. P. Davis, Mrs. Elizabeth Sims, Mrs. Geo. F. Koon, Mrs. C. W. McNair, Mrs. S. A. Ackerman, Mr. and Mrs. C. E. Flick, Mrs. E. Garner, Mrs. J. W. Phelps, Miss Edith Davis and C. M. Chambers.

These persons were summoned to meet at the house of John Dale, July, 1886, for the purpose of organizing a class. J. W. Phelps, presiding elder, was present, and authorized the proceedings. This beginning was made before even a public hall in the vicinity could be found in which to assemble, and all meetings were held in private residences. Mr. Dale, himself a preacher of good gifts, could instruct pertaining to the religious life, and held the little class together for the time being. But he was restless till more was done for the welfare of those composing the nucleus of a Church, as well as for the community of people in the neighborhood. Soon, however, he began planning and executing, and by the help of the presiding elder and C. W. Savidge (the latter at that time pastor of the First Church) seconding Mr. Dale's proposals, a lot was purchased at the north-west corner of Georgia and Woolworth avenues.

Nothing had been done towards determining the ability of the Society to purchase a lot or rear a house in which to worship. The three brethren before mentioned borrowed at the bank $300 to make the first payment on the lot. But a subscription to build a church was nearly at once presented for signatures, and the Methodists of the city, without regard to location, responded liberally. A contract was let to build, and the outcome was the tasty little house costing $3,600 that for five years adorned the corner of those prominent avenues. It was a credit to its projectors and an immense help to the people within reach of its influence. On the seventh of March, 1887, the house was dedicated by Rev. Joseph W. Phelps, and nearly enough of money had been pledged, including the sums previously secured, to pay for it.

In effecting a complete organization the first Board of Trustees was made up of John Dale, J. M. Chambers, J. F. Dale and O. P. McCarty; and the original Stewards were Mrs. Mary A. Davis, Mrs. John Dale, John L. Wilkie, C. E. Flick, John Dale, W. S. Marr and David I. Hayden. On the day of dedication a Sunday-school was organized, and John Dale was elected Superintendent.

At the session of the Annual conference, October, 1886, H. H. Millard was appointed pastor of this Church, and, though without a house in

which to preach for the first half of the year, he did
helpful work, and proved himself a faithful and
earnest religious tutor.   He received $1,000 for
his services.

One year later Geo. M. Brown was given the

REV. GEORGE M. BROWN.

pastoral oversight of the charge, in which office he
labored for five consecutive years.   The growth
of the Society in numbers and efficiency during his
pastorate is attributable, first, to his watchful care

of its interests, his mingling with the people, and his ability to organize co-operation, as well as to instruct from the pulpit. And, secondly, the increasing population in the contiguous parts of town, some of whom presented letters of membership.

The new, convenient and well furnished building that had been made ready for use six months before his coming gave him a fair opportunity to get a hearing on the vital questions affecting the weal of his auditors in this world and the world to come. He wielded the truths of the gospel with great candor and dexterity, making it clear and impressive, and won many to accept it. The membership was increased under his administration till two hundred and eighty-six names were enrolled, more than ninety of whom had been received on probation.

Almost immediately after Mr. Brown's appointment, the Society built a desirable preacher's house at an expense of $2,000, which has since been improved, till it is now one of the best in the Conference. This Church owes to him and his thoughtful wife the credit of being largely instrumental in the rapid and substantial improvement attending its early history.

The Society had so quickly accumulated a large number of communicants that, in 1892, near the expiration of Mr. Brown's term, for want of room, a new church-building enterprises was undertaken. Plans for a much larger and more costly structure were procured, examined and adopted. In a short time a contract was entered into, materials were purchased and workmen began the construction of a new edifice. The original house was moved from its site across the street to a vacant lot, and was used till the completion of the new one on the same lot before occupied by the old one. Like a generous people is capable of doing, the old building was donated to the Society at Walnut Hill which, up to this date, had been worshiping in a hired hall.

The inhabitants of this wealth-increasing district are deserving the thanks of the city for their enterprise in putting up such a large, well-designed and expensive church. It was dedicated February 25th, 1893. The cost of the house, with furnishings complete, was scarcely less than $35,000; and their property—grounds and buildings—is estimated at the sum of $40,000. But, as is too often the case, it is encumbered with a large debt. Yet the people are hopeful that, on the return of better times, it will be canceled.

This Society is in labors abundant in tutoring the children and youth in their flourishing Sunday-school, of which James Boyle is the present and active superintendent; and in encouraging their admirable Epworth League organization, which is claimed to be one of the best in the state, and in which great pride is taken by both the older and younger people of the Church.

At the close of Mr. Brown's pastorate in 1892,
W. P. Murray was transferred from the Erie Conference to take charge of this busy congregation.
He is young, but has sterling acquired ability,
studious, and an acceptable preacher and pastor.

The new church building occupies a very
sightly position being at the top of the hill on
Woolworth avenue, which terminates at Twenty-
ninth street. It faces Twenty-ninth street, extending back nearly seventy-five feet, having the main
entrance to the auditorium on the corner of the
building. Entering this the visitor finds himself
in a large ante-room formed by the sides of the
tower situated on the south-west corner of the
church. The interior of the building is finished in
light oak natural wood, and no pains have been
spared to make the church a cheery and pleasant
place in which to worship. The seats are of the
same material, arranged as an amphitheatre, and
cushioned with corduroy. Behind the congregation and occupying the space between the two
towers is a gallery capable of holding one hundred
and fifty persons which can be utilized when
necessary for a chorus choir or otherwise.

The pipe organ which is situated in an alcove
constructed for it just in the rear of the pulpit, is
one of the finest and best made of its kind in the
city, although not the costliest. It contains over
1,000 pipes and is finished in light oak to harmonize with the church itself.

To the left of the pulpit is a small door which leads to the pastor's study, a cozy room eight feet by twenty, occupying the south-east corner of the building. It has two large windows commanding a view to the south and east. To the right of the pulpit is a room for committee and like meetings.

The basement of the church is convenience itself for the purposes for which it is intended. The main apartment is the Sunday-school or lecture room which will seat comfortably four hundred people. It is seated with movable and very comfortable chairs which in the sessions of the Sunday-school can be arranged to suit the superintendent. On the west of the main room are two class rooms seating from seventy-five to one hundred each, divided from the main room by windows which are raised and lowered as the case requires. This is also the arrangement of the primary department on the east side of the main room. This will seat nearly two hundred people and is furnished with small chairs for the use of the primary scholars. In this room the Epworth League business and devotional meetings are held. It is also used as a dining room for church socials and in this particular its convenience is mostly appreciated. Directly to the south of this room is the pantry of the church provided with shelving and a large sink with the usual attachments. Behind this is the large kitchen, which in its turn is furnished with the conveniences incident to a well-ordered culinary department, including a gas stove.

Between the two class rooms on the west side of the basement is the hall and stairway leading to the auditorium above. This is made wide and easy of ascent the exits therefrom being into the two towers of the building. The entire building is heated by steam.

Another feature worthy of notice is the lighting arrangement which is by gas and so contrived that the whole building can be made one great blaze of light upon the hill-top. The main auditorium is lighted by one hundred and twenty jets on nine chandeliers and two brackets. Equal provision for light is made in the lecture room and class rooms.

CHAPTER VII.

EARLY in 1887 a movement was made in the north part of the city for the purpose of determining the feasibility of organizing a Society of our people in that promising addition to Omaha known as Kountze Place. The first meeting having in view such an attempt, as well as to formulate a plan of procedure, was held April 8th, 1887, at which time a Board of Trustees was appointed, composed of C. W. Cain, E. A. Parmelee, J. J. McLain, L. P. Pruyn and H. H. Miller; and articles of incorporation were prepared and filed.

In canvassing the question as to a site for a church building, Herman Kountze, the owner of lots that had been laid out, was solicited to donate a parcel of ground on which to erect a house of worship. John P. Roe interested himself in the project and was the instance, by personal persistence, in securing lots 6 and 7, in block 4, as a gratuity from the owner, and at the same time volunteered his services to aid in the enterprise by subscribing $500, made payable on condition nine others would each pledge an equal sum. With earnestness the soliciting was now begun with the purpose of holding Rev. Mr. Roe's subscription; the result of which effort, after some delay, secured the requisite number of subscribers, namely, Rev.

Dr. Maxfield, Geo. P. Bemis, J. Phipps Roe, M. M. Hamlin, L. A. Harmon, F. B. Brayton, H. H. Miller, A. H. Henry, A. T. Rector, and the Ladies' Aid Society.

T. B. Hilton, a late transfer, did some missionary work in the vicinity, but was soon relieved to accept a better appointment. J. E. Ensign at this juncture was engaged to procure subscriptions and to scan the neighborhood in searching for those who might be induced to take part in making up a class as well as to help in the erection of a church. Failing to obtain a guarantee of $1,200 as a salary, he resigned, leaving the parties interested in a quandary.

In the autumn of 1887, A. H. Henry was appointed to Castellar street, and finding and reporting the prospects dubious at that point, Bishop Fowler changed him to Trinity, which as yet had no organized Society. He willingly consented, and at once made preparations to take charge of the work. He actively entered upon the discharge of duty and organized the first class, November 13th, which comprised the following names: M. M. Hamlin, wife and three children, Ed. A. Parmelee and wife, Mrs. Nora H. Lemon, C. W. Cain and wife, and daughter Stella, J. J. McLain and wife, J. J. Toms and wife, L. A. Harmon and wife, O. T. Smith and wife, H. H. Miller, Mrs. F. B. Brayton, J. H. Cornes, C. D. Simms and wife, Elizabeth Hamilton. Edward

Bell, wife and family, Mrs. Willett, Mary Willett, Kittie Snow and Kate Elsas.

Soliciting subscriptions was kept up till the opening of spring, when a contract for building was effected with Mr. F. B. Brayton, at the corner henceforward known as Twenty-first and Binney streets. In the meantime, and after the organization of the Society, a brick store at the north-east corner of Twenty-fourth and Binney was hired and used as a place of holding religious services. As early as July, 1888, the Society began using the lecture room of the new church as a place of worship, even before the slate was on the roof. The mechanics made haste in preparing the main house for occupation; and it was completed in time for the dedication on Sunday, October 28th, Bishop Newman preaching in the morning and Rev. R. N. McKaig in the evening, when the house was formally dedicated to the worship of God.

The cost of the building aggregated $17,500, and of this sum there was owing about $7,000 at the date first above named, all of which was pledged on that day, practically clearing the Society of debt, except a loan of $4,000 from the Church Extension Society. The location of the house is central and conspicuous, in the midst of one of the most pleasant residence portions of the town. A condition in the sale of lots excluding the establishment of saloons, and requiring that

no purchaser would be permitted to build a residence costing less than $2,500, has effected the
building up of a choice place for homes.

The dimensions of the main edifice including
only the auditorium are sixty-six by sixty-six feet;
and along the south side, but under the same roof.
is a two-story lecture room twenty-eight by sixty-
six feet. The walls are of brick, and the internal
trimmings are of southern pine finished in natural
color. A heavy-looking square tower is built in
the north-west corner of the structure through
which is the main entrance to the audience room.
The great doors between the auditorium and the
lecture room are hung on weights admitting of
their being lowered so as to throw both rooms
together when occasion requires. The floor
inclines towards the pulpit, and is filled with
approved opera chairs, providing seats for nearly
four hundred.

The erection, completion and occupancy of
this extensive sanctuary in a new portion of town
was a matter of momentous interest at that time,
and has been ever since a source of pleasure to
those who conceived the enterprise and continue
to enjoy the privileges it affords.

A Sunday-school was organized November
13th, 1887, with H. H. Miller, Superintendent, and
six teachers, Rev. J. P. Roe, E. A. Parmelee,
Mrs. Nora Lemon, Miss Fanny Bell, Jessie Bell
and the pastor, A. H. Henry, and forty scholars.

And at the taking possession of the new church
and better quarters, at once the numbers and usefulness were augmented.

In the pastoral office the following have served
at the dates given and in the order in which their

REV. JOHN W. ROBINSON, D. D.

names occur. A. H. Henry from October, 1887,
to September, 1888. He saw the new edifice in
all the stages of progress from the laying of the
foundation till nearing its completion. His allow-

ance was $700 as an unmarried man. J. W. Robinson was his immediate successor, and remained one year, receiving as a salary $1,200, not including house rent of $30 per month. At this period, September, 1889, the Sunday-school numbered one hundred and thirty, and the membership had increased to one hundred and eighty, showing that Mr. Robinson's year's work had produced no small measure of favorable results. He enjoyed and gave much time to his books, was clear and concise in his preaching, and in the prayer meeting thoroughly at home and forceful. As an instructor in the religious life he was capable of setting forth duty so distinctly as not to be gainsaid. With all his powers he believed the revelation of truth, and that the holy Book is inspired. No duty that he was able to perform was too burdensome; and he was always anxious to be used in leading souls to Christ. He was not a theological adventurer, but adhered to the doctrines as set forth in the twenty-five Articles of faith.

The steady-going and correct W. K. Beans followed next to the pastorate of Trinity, and for five successive years, or, from September, 1889, to October, 1894, with but brief intermissions during the heat of summer, continuously was at his post of duty. During this long term, which is the lawful limit of service in the same charge, the membership was increased one hundred per cent., and he reported at the expiration of his pastorate two hundred and fifty. And the charge in every other respect is doubly efficient in carrying on Church work.

In the five years there were expended in improving the property $1,000, including architectural changes, interior decorations, heightening the smoke stack, improving the furnace, grading, sodding, stone steps and walk and street paving. Toward the payment of debt there were raised in cash and subscriptions $7,500; and for each of four years in benevolent collections it was the banner charge of the Conference !

.On Mr. Beans' coming to Nebraska he was first stationed at Eighteenth Street Church, Omaha, three years; next at Nebraska City, three years; three years at Beatrice, where he built the beautiful Centenary church, one of the finest in Methodism. He was then appointed to York district, and after one year as presiding elder was made pastor at York, where remaining a year he was transferred to Trinity Church, Omaha. His work at York was characterized by an awakening when three hundred were converted.

Each of the last three years at Trinity, Mr. Beans' salary was $2,000, and his labors with these people who sustained him so cheerfully resulted in cementing the membership and perpetuating a vigorous society. Mr. Beans was transferred to Salt Lake in June, 1895.

Dr. F. H. Sanderson, a transfer from the Northwest Iowa Conference, was appointed to this interesting charge, October, 1894. Since his coming the regular services were interrupted for a

REV. F. H. SANDERSON, D. D.

time on account of making extensive repairs to the building. The auditorium was made even better than before, and, with other changes, cost nearly the sum of $3,000.

Dr. Sanderson is a native of Canada, and comes with approved credentials after serving thirteen years in the Conference whence he came. He occupied, during his ministry in Iowa, some of the leading pulpits of the Conference, and had built up a reputation as a pulpit and platform speaker. His election to the presidency of the Iowa State Epworth League, and his having served nine years as Secretary of his Conference, signify his effectiveness as well as the esteem in which he was held by his former associates. He received the degree of D.D. from Cornell College, Iowa, in recognition of his literary attainments.

The indebtedness on their property, including that to the Church Extension Society, part of which was occasioned by an unexpected happening that no business forecast could apprehend, is not very embarrassing. And before the occurrence of many equinoxes very likely the Trustees will make provision for its cancellation.

The Sunday-school, with Allen T. Rector at its head, is more than usually alive and interesting. It is composed of thirty officers and teachers and an enrollment of two hundred and fifty scholars, and an average attendance of two hundred and ten. The average annual expense is about $200 in purchasing supplies, such as books, papers and periodicals, and all other requisites.

SOUTH OMAHA is regarded as an adjunct of the metropolis; and the Church, with some showing of right, is, at this time, and on this page, enumerated with other suburban Churches. The town is built upon a site part of which a decade since was cultivated grain fields. Its origin and growth have been mainly owing to the establishment of stock yards and packing houses. A village was laid out, and the settling of new comers began at once, among them, as is always the case in the West, a few Methodists; and before others were aware of his presence, a preacher was among them taking in the prospect. The growth of the suburb was from the beginning very rapid, entitling it to the name of "Magic City."

In September, 1886, T. B. Hilton, by assignment, became pastor of a charge yet to be made in South Omaha, who soon organized a class of five members, namely, J. A. Silver, Mr. and Mrs. White, Mrs. Lucy Shriver and Mrs. E. L. Crawford, thus commencing a work that has been gaining through all the years since that date. Mr. Hilton accomplished the building of a small chapel and parsonage during the year, and from this almost insignificant commencement the large and flourishing Society of to-day has resulted. The site of the church and parsonage was about thirty-five feet above the present grade at the north-east corner of Twenty-third and N streets. The cost of these structures was very nearly $1,300. The parsonage, which is still in use as the preacher's house, having been taken down off the bank, added to and repaired, originally cost about $400.

To effect the building of these houses at the date of its having been done was accomplished by the audacious pastor's industry and determination. He planned and executed with a skilful head and energetic hand.

The first board of Trustees was constituted of Rev. T. B. Hilton, James A. Silver, Isaac Earl and Wm. White. The composition means a scarcity of material for such use, both in respect of the pastor's having to serve and the small number constituting the board. But it was a success to be the instrument at that day of making as comfortable provision for the people to worship and as good a shelter for the pastor's family, though only a small sum was required for the purpose of their erection.

The following year, September, 1887, L. H. Eddleblute was given charge of the small number who congregated in the little chapel, and removed his family into the no more seemly parsonage close by its side. But these were the days of small things at South Omaha, and the preacher had to sacrifice in a measure both comfort and convenience; and the willingness to be humble was part of the explanation of his being able to nurture the flock and witness its prosperity.

But Mr. Eddleblute ascertained the following spring that the authorities of the city intended cutting the streets to grade, by the doing of which an ascent of such hight to the Church would render it inaccessible to many, immediately after consulting his friends, set about planning for a larger and more costly place of worship to be located on the same corner but on the street level. The old church was disposed of for a trifling sum and the proceeds were appropriated to the new enterprise.

Mr. Eddleblute remained in charge two years, and the young city the while was rapidly increasing in population and wealth, but his staying was not long enough to see the new edifice finished. He had wrought industriously in securing cash and pledges, and was pleased to witness the walls being reared, but was unable to push the work so as to allow of his occupying it as a preaching place before the expiration of his term. The Church Extension Society granted a loan to assist in the expense of construction. which was a great help in encouraging the undertaking.

The new house was, when completed, a substantial edifice with a brick basement for a Sunday-school room, and, besides, a class room. The auditorium above was frame, and had floor area to furnish seating for two hundred and fifty.

The new building cost $4,000, and was none too large nor roomy for the demand almost at once made on its capacity. During Mr. E.'s term the Society almost reached the point of self-support. His salary the second year was $700, and fully met, and he reported a membership of eighty-five.

In September, 1889, David Marquette succeeded to the pastorate, only remaining one year, when he was removed to take charge of the Elkhorn Valley district. During his stay, however, the new church was completed, dedicated and paid for excepting the loan of $1,000 from the Church Extension Society. The increasing population and the growth of the membership soon began crowding the house. The number of members had now reached one hundred and seven, and the promise of additions favorable.

The laborious and enterprising pastor had seen the new house made ready for use, and enjoyed preaching from its pulpit to a congregation of intelligent people. Indeed the last two pastors had done for South Omaha and Methodism by persistent industry that which was not only creditable to their business ability, but likewise that which was the means of giving character and prestige to the denomination which they represented.

C. N. Dawson was transferred from South Tenth Street Church, Omaha, to this charge, September, 1890, and having successfully served elsewhere had some assurance of being able with equal

chances to promote the Society here. He had no
competition in the ministry coming from preachers
of our own denomination; but there was an open
field and a rarely good prospect. Using his
resources, he soon perceived favorable indications.

REV. CHARLES N. DAWSON, D. D.

After spending twelve months and more, and
by this time becoming acquainted with the wants
and ability of his people, he judged an effort
should be made to free the Church of debt; and on

the 26th of June, 1892, he presented the matter to
his congregation, asking and getting $1,500. This
was regarded a triumph, and henceforth gave
impetus to every feature of the work. But the
rejoicing was not of long lasting, for on the 18th
of January following the sanctuary was destroyed
by fire. In about six years the Society by the help
of friends and business men had built two churches,
and now must contrive the erection of the third.

The burning of the house aroused very general
public sympathy in behalf of the Society, and a
lively interest was taken in the new movement.
Men and women subscribed liberally, and the
pastor partaking of the spirit of the people was
confident of being able to provide a new place of
worship suited to the demands of the public.
During the interval of twelve months, including
the time of the destruction of the one building till
the occupancy of the other, the congregation worshiped in the hall of the Knights of Pythias. But
the foundation of the new edifice was built and the
walls were raised to such height as to be in readiness for the corner stone which was a donation
from Drexel & Son, of Omaha. On the 9th of
July, 1893, the stone was laid with ceremonies,
Frank Crane delivering the address on the occasion. The Church Extension Society came oppor-
tunely to their help again with a loan, and a gift of
$500. All things seemed to combine in giving
courage to the projectors, and good progress was

made in the execution of the mechanical work till the house was finished.

The site of the new building is the same as that on which the former church stood. The structure stands fronting south, is fifty feet wide and seventy feet in length, and a tower twelve feet square and seventy-six in hight ornaments the south-west corner which serves as a vestibule. The basement is of brick and arranged to accommodate the Sunday-school, prayer and social meetings. The lecture room has capacity to seat one hundred and eighty; a class room on the north side seats sixty, and on the west are two each of which seats fifty. On the south is the infant's room holding fifty. The smaller rooms all open into the lecture room by means of sliding doors. A pastor's study, kitchen and store room are also on this floor, making an arrangement nearly faultless.

The auditorium on the second floor is inclosed by wooden walls and roofed with sharp hips and steep valleys cutting it into several angles which give the building a modern perspective and pleasing to the eye. The room is large and airy making it as agreeable as skill is capable. The floor inclines towards the pulpit and is seated with comfortable pews for five hundred. The internal trimming is of ash finished in old copper.

The day of dedication was anticipated with extreme solicitude and interest. The date was fixed for January 21st, 1895, and observed. It was eventful to South Omaha Methodists. The church was filled; even more than the pews could hold turned out to mingle with the throng and share in the grateful service. Frank Crane delivered an inspiring gospel discourse. after which the pastor asked for $1,250, and in a few minutes the entire sum was subscribed. The cost of the building and furniture is $10,000, and the property of the Society is valued at $17,000.

The present membership is three hundred and fifty, and is increasing by frequent accessions. Their ability to maintain a pastor and his family by contributing to his support a sum sufficient for a living is not now questioned. The outlook is in every way hopeful. After a pastoral term of five years, now soon to expire, Mr. Dawson will leave to his successor a charge to be desired by any itinerant who seeks to be useful.

The Sunday-school is not large, but is well cared for by efficient officers and teachers. The enrollment of scholars is one hundred and seventy-five, and the school is superintended by W. A. McCollister. Since 1890 two others have been at its head in turn, namely, E. M. Richardson and E. D. Gideon.

A thriving Epworth League is in active work taking part in all that pertains to the advancement of morals and religion. The membership of the League is one hundred and fifteen.

CHAPTER IX.

BUILDING and settling this suburb began as early as 1886, and before the next year closed as many houses and barns had been erected as to make a showing like a new village on the east hillside. In keeping an outlook for opportunity, a Methodist preacher was promptly on the ground seeking an open door. Early in the year of 1888, Wm. B. Slaughter, Jr., preached at the house of Walter B. Prugh, Thirty-fourth street and Fowler avenue, to his family and some of his neighbors, and at intervals thereafter. Several times, at the instance of T. C. Clendening, others ministered repeatedly to these people, among them John P. Roe, John Dale, Albert Rose, A. L. Stonecypher and the author.

In the summer of 1888 a lot was donated by the Monmouth Park Building Association, of which party another lot was purchased at a cost of $750. These parcels of ground comprised a site for a house of worship; and a church building was contemplated even before a class was organized, on account of the seeming need of the citizens. Antedating this period, and to be ready when the need of such officers might occur, a board of Trustees was elected at a Quarterly conference held at

A. M. Clark's residence in West Omaha, in the winter of 1888, as follows: Everett Ball, A. D. Brown, G. L. Bellows, J. T. Coleman, C. F. Cunningham, W. B. Prugh and O. J. Stevenson.

The Presiding Elder was most active in accomplishing the results that followed such preparation; and felt warranted in the attempt to build after securing a donation of the Church Extension Society of $250, and a loan of an equal sum. Subscriptions were solicited, though little was effected in that way in getting aid. A neat and comfortable frame church was begun and its construction soon completed at a cost of about $2,200, with capacity to seat two hundred and twenty people.

On January 22d, 1889, the Society was incorporated. The names of the incorporators are, T. C. Clendening, (the presiding elder,) G. M. Brown, W. B. Slaughter, J. H. Coffman, Martin L. Plotts and Walter B. Prugh. The interest in the project increased as the approach to completion was witnessed, and the approaching date of dedicating the new house added to the pleasure of all concerned.

The day came, and the indebtedness on the house and lot amounted to $1,800. March 6th, 1889, was epochal in the history of the Society. Bishop Newman preached the dedicatory discourse, and received subscriptions, pledges and cash to the amount of $1,050. The remaining

$750 was secured by giving a mortgage on the prop-
erty which has since been lifted as well as reducing
the loan from the Church Extension Society.

The names of those composing the first class
were, Everett Ball, Mrs. E. Ball, G. H. Bellows,
Rebecca Bellows, A. D. Brown and wife, Mrs.
S. W. Bliss and Emma Goodyear.

Previously, and in the fall of 1888, W. B.
Slaughter, Jr., was regularly appointed to the
Omaha circuit which included Monmouth Park.
His labors at the outset without a house of worship to which the people might be invited, seemed
to produce very little impression, though he attentively met his appointments and mingled with the
people in an effort to promote practical religion.
Several months ensued before he had the use of
the new building; and from the date of its completion till the year's end he was annoyed with the
indifference of the inhabitants in regard to attending the house of worship. But he endeavored to
hold the little band together in hopes of the coming of a better day. The statistics show that in
the entire circuit there could be counted only forty
members, and of probationers, thirty-four. He
received for his twelve month's work $400.

Before the ending of his term, A. L. Mickel, a
student from college, came to Omaha to spend
vacation, and did some preaching at Monmouth
Park, and later became a member of the North
Nebraska Conference.

The next year the work was left to be supplied. A person of the name of Manuel was put in charge, who had not the art of pleasing, and by the time of the coming of the second quarter absented himself, remaining only long enough to be entitled to one-fourth of the Missionary appropriation for the current year.

By request of the presiding elder John P. Roe now took charge of the work at Monmouth Park, only, and served to the end of the Conference year. A debt on the premises was still annoying the membership, and Mr. Roe proposed as far as he could to relieve the Society of obligations requiring the payment of money. He offered to serve without pay, and made a present of $75 of missionary money set apart for this charge for that year. He soon learned of small bills owing to different parties for the payment of which he made provision as far as possible, though the ability of the few to discharge debts was not considerable.

Mr. Roe's greatest success was in securing the payment of debts, and he chose this opportunity to free them, if possible. But he faithfully and regularly preached to the congregation that assembled weekly to hear the truth presented. And the hearers will hardly forget some of the lessons he taught, nor the eloquence of his words as he interpreted the law and the gospel. He did a praiseworthy work, and in a way that few can afford, by giving his time and services without compensation; and by thus doing held the Church together, and encouraged the people to make advancement in the religious life.

He reported at the year's end eighteen members and seven probationers, and a Sunday-school

REV. FRANK W. BROSS.

of thirty pupils; as well as the church building and ground at $3,200, as the estimated value of their property.

In September, 1890, F. W. Bross was appointed

to this charge which still included other points. He began his labors with a zeal commendable, regarding himself as commissioned to evangelize the community. His labors were so owned of God that a change for the better was wrought the first year, very much to the credit of the pastor and to the good cheer of the membership. Living at Monmouth Park, that Society received a larger share of his attention, and was depended upon for more than an equal share of his salary. His fidelity and unpretentious efforts were approved of all men, and to the present his humble life is mentioned as half the battle in winning success.

Mr. Bross remained three years during which the work was divided, and the last year his time was all spent at the Park and West Omaha. An appropriation of $200 was made for the work the first year of his having charge, but was reduced to $50 the last year. These sums were helpful in subsisting his family. The third year he received $420 for his services, and $96 for house rent, making a total of $516. He was the instance of organizing an Epworth League that flourished in his care; also the Sunday-school of eighty scholars and teachers was prosperous. He reports the membership at seventy-three, and of probationers, nine. This showing is indicative of progress, and with good attention this charge will soon be numbered with the desirable fields in Omaha.

Mr. Bross's removal in the autumn of 1893 gave

place to T. W. Mathews, who was appointed as his successor to serve the one point, now made a station. He was reappointed in 1894, and while his labors have not been well rewarded in dollars and cents, he and his family have been sustained in some measure of comfort. For his first year's services he received from the Church $260, and for the payment of house rent $72, besides an appropriation of $50 of Missionary money.

The violent reverses in business in the past two years, curtailing the earnings of so large a proportion of the people, work a hardship on the pastor of a small station. But Mr. Mathews in good heart is cheerfully making the best of the situation, while his people desire his welfare and are making honest endeavors to support him at least in comfort.

The spiritual interests of the charge are cared for on the pastor's part with diligence, and the class meetings and prayer services are enlivened by the joyous experience of some of the most devoted members. And from the pulpit is heard only the gospel in its integrity, not vauntingly but in respect to its serious and gracious provisions. The work in spite of all the obstacles is gradually improving, and this year will, most likely, be decisive of the practicability of making this point a station, with $100 of a missionary appropriation.

At the Conference of 1894, or the ending of

this pastor's first year, he reported a membership of sixty-nine, and a Sunday-school of nearly one hundred pupils; also a Senior and Junior League, both advancing.

Some fault is found with part of the population of the community on account of their irreverent way of spending the Sabbath. The gospel's reforming effect must work a change before this Society shall reach the point of its greatest influence.

Mr. Mathews' second year is imposing heavy burdens upon him and his people so far as support and supporting can affect them. But he uncomplainingly is laboring as if he had the heritage of a prince.

CHAPTER X.

THE story of Methodism in West Omaha begins as elsewhere—in the Sunday-school. In the year 1876 A. M. Clark donated a piece of ground at the present corner of Thirty-seventh and Marcy streets, on which to build a small house then in contemplation, in which to hold religious services. The site at that date was not inside the city limits, but several Methodists either had or soon afterwards made homes in the vicinity, among them Harrison Johnson and family, A. M. Clark and wife, O. B. Seldon and wife, A. H. Doneken and wife; and these were soon followed by Dr. W. B. Slaughter with his wife and daughter, Hattie. All of these, however, except Dr. Slaughter, held their membership in town. Mrs. A. M. Clark, another daughter of Dr. Slaughter, was too much interested in the moral welfare of her own household and of the children of the neighborhood to delay making efforts for their good. Accordingly she offered room in her home for the assembling of the young people that they might be taught from the word of God. This beginning resulted in the organization of a Sunday-school which was kept up in this way for a year, and the increasing attendance made a demand for more room.

In the spring of 1878 a small building, eighteen by twenty-eight feet, was erected on the ground that had been donated by Mr. Clark, as a provision for the Sunday-school. Soon as the house was ready it was occupied by the school, which prospered for a time, but for the want of efficient officers and teachers eventually was given up. The Methodists of the neighborhood, still maintaining their membership in the old First Church in the city, were too much disposed to attend services with the great congregation rather than give much heed to the small affair in the suburbs.

During the intervening ten years beginning with 1878 preaching services were freqently held in the little church. Local and other preachers supplied the pulpit without charge for a few years, part of the time keeping up regular appointments. At a later date I. A. Bradrick, a superannuated member of the Iowa Conference, whose home was now in Omaha, was given charge, but on account of impaired health soon relinquished it. T. B. Hilton, a transfer from Illinois, accepted charge, but, for the want of adequate support, continued but a short time. In the meantime a class was organized, which, for want of attention, was shortly disbanded.

The explanation of all the failures at this place is in there being no one ready to make as much sacrifice as was required to perpetuate a Society that needed nurturing. Patient attention by a few ardent and interested men and women possessing such gifts as to pray, lead a class or superintend a Sunday-school, would have been the means of building up a congregation and all the services in West Omaha long since.

A class was again organized when W. B. Slaughter, jr., took charge of the work, by appointment, in 1888; and during his term as much progress was made as to enumerate over twenty-five members, and a Sunday-school of some promise was resuscitated. Mr. Slaughter's labors, though a licentiate in the ministry, resulted in giving impetus to the work in contrast with the unsteady efforts that had hitherto been made in behalf of the Society, but the sum contributed towards his support was a moiety.

In 1890, Charles Snavely succeeded to the charge still embracing other points at which he preached. A small missionary appropriation was made in his behalf which helped to subsist him. He was both active and popular, and gave still greater encouragement to the membership, though his stay was but one year. The following year Geo. S. Davis, who had been one of the proprietors and editors of the *Nebraska Christian Advocate*, supplied the work for about six months. The wavering Society grew under his labors, and such a regimen would have secured still greater prosperity if he had remained. But he had offered his services to the Missionary Society to go to a foreign field, and was appointed at this date as superintendent of the Bulgarian Mission in Eastern Europe.

Mr. Davis's place at West Omaha was filled by J. E. Miller, who very soon left the work, and the brief remainder of the year was filled by T. C. Blatchley. These frequent changes in the pastorate were anything but helpful to the charge, as neither the preacher or people was benefited.

At the session of the Conference of 1892. Charles Snavely was returned, after an absence of one year, and divided his time between four preaching places included in the field. The work was kept intact, but little advancement was apparent. In 1893 F. Tonge, an Englishman, was appointed. He had the ability of fluent speech, but was without a liking for itinerating on such a field, which at this time included also Benson Place. His personal appearance and manners, though a good talker did not captivate the people, and he accomplished very little for the work, yet he continued to the year's end.

The cutting down process was applied again, and West Omaha was left alone to support a pastor —a suburban station with a small church building and a correspondingly small membership, offering a prospect not in the least flattering to an ambitious young preacher.

Farnum Ellis, with little previous experience,

was appointed, and assumed charge. Possessing health and courage, he entered upon the task of raising up a self-supporting Church, excepting an appropriation by the Missionary Society about sufficient for his living one-fourth of the year. The prospect was not auspicious, for he found but seven claiming a membership, most of whom were

REV. FARNUM ELLIS.

women—determined, praying women. With these he entered into covenant to plead with God for success in saving souls, almost leaving out the question of support for himself and his little family.

Only a few months had elapsed when showers of mercy began falling, and long before the first year had ended he had enrolled more than fifty additional names. The services were held part of the year in a vacant store at Thirty-fifth and Leavenworth streets, "and at the mid-winter revival," says Bro. Ellis, "more than sixty souls bowed at the altar, most of whom testified to God's saving power." This gave to the workers new life, and endued then with even greater determination to wage a warfare of conquest, in spite of the disadvantage at which they wrought.

At this juncture it was decided that a better place of worship must be provided. And, during the summer, the attempt was made by turning the little chapel at Thirty-seventh and Marcy streets half way around, and during the fall a commodious and well-finished addition of twenty-six by thirty feet was put up at the south end of the old structure that the room afforded by both might be used. A tower was constructed at the east front through which an entrance is made to the auditorium by passing vestibule doors. The main room is cut off from the lecture chapel by means of folding doors. The property is now estimated to be worth $3.000. The taste in planning and finishing the edifice is due in part to Mr. John Widenor, who took interest in effecting the improvement. The house will now accommodate two hundred people with easy opera chairs. It is heated by a furnace and lighted with gas.

To accomplish the fitting up of this nearly new

place of worship imposed a heavy burden on the hard working pastor. But the fatigue of soliciting money and donations of whatever he could obtain that would contribute to success, he considered as nothing in comparison of effecting his object. His desire to provide a place where people might worship in comfort was paramount, and the object was accomplished. The house was dedicated October 14th, 1894, by Dr. J. B. Maxfield, presiding elder, at which service a collection was taken nearly sufficient to cover all indebtedness.

But the work of good results did not cease with the occupancy of the new place of worship. The tireless preacher, now spending the second year with these people, during the winter of 1894-5, with the occasional aid of some of the city pastors, carried on another revival meeting which was the means of awakening a gracious religious interest. And an addition of nearly fifty to the membership resulted.

The Trustees are A. L. Stonecypher, William Peak, John Lewis, John Widenor, George Cornell, Joseph Nobes and George Irey; and the Stewards are, namely, Graham Park, jr., Edward Clark, M. G. Edwards, Mrs. Jane Fuller, Mrs. J. Russell and Miss Mary Peak; Superintendent of Sunday-school, C. W. Florkee; President of Epworth League, Miss Mary Peak; Class Leader, A. M. Clark.

Altogether, this charge is promising a harvest

of fruitage that eventually will make it a desirable field of labor; and if given good culture will, at an early day, sustain a pastor creditably.

This year, even during the summer, the attendance at worship is large enough to encourage the pastor and friends. The new house has brought about a great change in attracting people, and the pastor is permitted to preach to more who appreciate the gospel than the former house would hold. Mr. Ellis will be able to make a good report at the coming Conference.

CHAPTER XI.

ALMOST without exception the beginning of Church work on the outskirts of the city was by opening a Sunday-school; and this rule applies to the West Side, now the South-west Church. On the 6th of May, 1888, a school of twenty-four pupils was organized under the pastorate of C. H. Savidge, father of Charles W., who himself for the time being, served as superintendent, with Miss Maggie Boniwitz as secretary. Mr. Savidge's circuit included Walnut Hill, West Omaha and West Side, each of which appointments now and alone sustains a pastor. The Sunday-school was held, by permission of the Board of Education of the city, in the West Side school house as also were the preaching services. A Society was organized at the home of Daniel Roberts; John Dale, C. H. Savidge and C. J. Roberts being mainly instrumental in effecting it.

Mr. Savidge's term included one year, when he was succeeded by Wm. B. Slaughter, jr., who also had charge but twelve months, and was left without an appointment to attend school. The young itinerant preached to old neighbors and associates of his boyhood and made a good impression. But his desire for more knowledge induced him to seek it at the great schools of Evanston, Illinois.

Charles Snavely was appointed to the charge, September, 1889, and efficiently co-operating with the people, soon was recognized as possessing qualities in excess of ordinary young men in the pulpit, and his frequent visits to the homes of his membership endeared him to the people. The Society's thrift under his administration is evidence of his efficiency. He gave promise of making a thorough and trustworthy pastor, and is since making good proof of his ministry on other fields of labor.

Following the appointment of Mr. Snavely Frank W. Bross is given charge in September of the next year. He was studiously a Methodist, and wrought to save souls, was companionable in his visits from house to house, particularly taking an interest in the religious welfare of the youth of the charge. If in the pulpit he was at any loss, he more than made it up in devotion to the interests of the work. Near the time of his accepting the appointment the Society was excluded from worshiping in the school-house by a resolution of the Board of Education. Thereafter, and till May, 1891, services were held in the West Lawn schoolhouse, outside of the city limits such a distance as to be a real disadvantage to the little band of determined co-workers. This inconvenience, however, was of short duration, and as soon as their new church was enclosed the faithful pastor began a revival meeting, and, as a result, a company of young converts was added.

In the meantime the building of a house of worship was projected. A lot was secured for a site near the corner of Fifty-first and Hickory streets. This location at that date was simply a country place. Subscriptions were obtained in such sums as to warrant the attempt to build, and late in the spring the house was finished and occupied to the great pleasure of the heroic Society which accomplished the result so helpful to the surrounding community. A Board of Trustees had been appointed as early as March, 1888, as follows: C. J. Roberts, G. A. Ritchey and G. S. Ambler to be ready when an effort might be made to build a place of worship. The Board at the present date consists of C. J. Roberts, John Blake, Geo. H. Syas, F. G. Davie and F. W. Young. The place of holding services now occupied, is a one-story frame structure, twenty-eight by fifty feet in dimensions, costing $1,400, and is very well arranged for the purposes for which it was erected. Usually it is well filled with a congregation on the Sabbath, and at the hour of Sunday-school a hive of children and youth assemble.

On June 28th, 1891, the dedicatory services were held, Rev. H. A. Crane, A. M., preaching the sermon, at which time the property was cleared of debt except a loan of $250 from the Church Extension Society. Indeed, no money was asked for at the dedication, and at this date the loan has all been paid but $100.

Charles Snavely was returned to this charge after an absence of one year and after the Society had been set off to itself to maintain a pastor without help from other points. Some trouble was experienced in acquiring support for him though he served the people popularly. But the charge was developing towards a self-sustaining condition; since which, with its increasing membership, gains are making in ability and influence.

Succeeding Mr. Snavely, J. Q. A. Fleharty served the charge for two years, during which term fifty-four were added to the membership. An Epworth League was organized with twenty-five members, Fletcher W. Young as president and Gertie Weaver as secretary. The League induced and holds together in attendance a number of young people, several of whom have been brought into membership in the Church.

An attack of illness, impairing his strength, was in Mr. Fleharty's way during the latter year of his term. But, notwithstanding, he held the respect of the people and continued his interest in the welfare of the charge. The chief men and women of the Society, among them Mr. C. J. Roberts, very efficiently aided in keeping up services both on the Sabbath and in the week time. As a preacher he is sound, instructive and devout. His former experience in the pastorate fitting him for the discernment of subjects for the pulpit adapted to his hearers and the occasion. He always aims to be helpful to any who are seeking or craving more light.

The Epworth League is of immense help to this Society, and has been mostly in charge of its able and sensible president and his wife, who have given much time and many prayers for its success. They are now being rewarded in seeing the young people taking part intelligently in the services of the Church and Sunday-school without timidity.

The Sunday-school with F. W. Young at its head, a Bible student and singer, is, like the Society, building up and prospering. Beginning a few years since with twenty-four scholars, it now numbers an enrollment of one hundred and thirty-nine! And it has a corps of eleven teachers, a small but select library and a full supply of lesson helps; "and taking numbers into the account, is the equal of any in the city in enthusiasm as well as the quantity and quality of work done."

The Southwest Church is evidently approach-ing a period of importance, and each succeeding year witnesses an improvement in all lines of Church work. Though its place of holding serv-ices is on the present frontier of the city, it is enumerated in the metropolitan appointments. In a few years, at most, if it continues to prosper, a large Society will take the place of the former small one, demanding, hence, the entire time and services of an every-way capable preacher and pastor.

Rev. Mr. Hopkins, a returned missionary, in October, 1894, was employed by the presiding elder to supply this work. He was a devoted christian and an able sermonizer, but it became necessary that he should change his residence, and in the spring the charge was left without a pastor. Early in the summer a late graduate of the Nebraska Wesleyan University, W. W. Shank, was placed in charge who is now serving acceptably.

CHAPTER XII.

EARLY in the autumn of 1890, T. C. Clendening and A. L. Stonecypher began agitating the establishment of a Mission in the vicinity of Fortieth and Hamilton streets, in Orchard Hill addition. After enlisting the interest of F. L. Cotton and family, Mr. and Mrs. Frank Johnson and others, a meeting was called to deliberate the matter. Nelson & Knight's hall was procured for that purpose, and when the people had assembled Mr. Clendening, the presiding elder, preached. This occurrence was of the date of Thanksgiving evening, 1890. Afterwards Geo. S. Davis, editor of the *Nebraska Advocate*, and John Dale preached in the same hall.

On Sunday morning, January 4th, 1891, Mr. Clendening, assisted by P. S. Merrill, pastor of the First Church, formally organized a Society of ten members, viz., Mr. and Mrs. F. L. Cotton, Miss Mattie Mason, Mr. and Mrs. Frank Johnson, Miss Eunice Stanardt, and Mr. and Mrs. A. L. Stonecypher. Mr. Merrill preached the inaugural discourse. In the evening services were held by G. M. Brown, pastor of Hanscom Park Church.

The first trustees were F. L. Cotton, Frank Johnson and A. L. Stonecypher. Thenceforth services were held with some regularity on the Sabbath, the preaching being done by different ones. John Dale, Mr. Lockwood, Dr. Sherwood, J. P. Roe and others, took turns at serving. The first revival meeting was conducted by D. F. Rodabaugh, in January, lasting two weeks.

To make certain and permanent the work already begun it was deemed necessary to secure the services of a pastor who might regularly preach to the people and take an oversight of the persons now attached to the class. Rev. T. C. Webster, of Kearney, Neb., by the solicitations of Mr. and Mrs. F. L. Cotton, was prevailed upon to accept the pastorate; and on June 15th, 1891, preached his first sermon. The membership in the interim had reached seventeen.

The meetings were held in the hall that was first hired; but in November the store room a little west of Lowe avenue, on the same street, was rented for a place of holding public services. By this time the membership had grown to such numbers that it was needful to make better provisions for their accommodation. A good deal of interest was taken in contriving to better their condition, till in the fall of 1892 the Official Board decided that a place of worship of their own must be provided. The Trustees began making arrangements for such an attempt.

This was an opportune time, for Hanscom Park church would soon be vacated, giving place to a new house. A committee was appointed to confer with the Trustees of the last named Church; and, by the intercession of John Dale of that Church, they were induced to donate the building to the Society at Wesley.

To make the furnishing themselves with a place of worship even more practicable, John P. Roe proffered a loan of $2,000 with which to purchase ground for a site. The proposal was accepted, and lots 12 and 13, block 3, Orchard Hill addition, were selected as the most desirable location, and were purchased. These lots are at the south-east corner of Forty-first and Charles streets, within one block of the Walnut Hill line of street cars.

Without the loss of much time a bargain was made to move the Hanscom Park church to the new place. But the expense of the removal and the cost of repairs incident to moving footed up very nearly $1,200, including a new foundation. When the building was ready for occupancy it presented the appearance of a decidedly comfortable house of worship. Bishop Bowman's services were secured to dedicate the now neat and desirable sanctuary, and on Sunday, April 10th, 1893, he preached to an interesting and expectant congregation from Acts xx, 35. A sum was raised at that time and since sufficient to clear the property of debt, except the money loaned by Mr. Roe with which to procure the site. The interest on the small indebtedness is also paid regularly.

That was a great day and occasion to the patrons and friends of Wesley Church; and the people through whose liberality and enterprise the event had been made possible felt abundantly rewarded in realizing that another place of worship had been added to the many already in use in the city, but more so because their families had pleasant sittings at a church of their own, and their Sunday-school had a place to hold its weekly sessions.

Mr. Webster, whose counsel and industry had largely contributed to this success, remained in charge till September of this year, having served as pastor for two years and three months. During his term the membership had been increased to eighty-seven, besides seven probationers. His ministry to the people on the hill had been immensely helpful, and he had occasion for rejoicing at the growth of the membership and the consequent importance of the new charge. He used every justifiable means in his reach to promote the cause of the Master. In discoursing he was practical, earnest and edifying. He was happy in his work, though his receipts in money were scanty and barely sufficient for his subsistence till the last year, when a salary of $1,000 was paid in instalments. From Wesley he was appointed to South Tenth street, Omaha, and in October, 1894, to Lyons.

T. C. Clendening, now having served a term on

the Omaha district, was appointed to succeed Mr.
Webster in September, 1893, and continued uninterruptedly till June of the next year, when he
accepted the agency of the Wesleyan University at
Lincoln, but remained in charge of Wesley Church

REV. JOHN E. MOORE.

till the meeting of the Annual conference, though
most of his working time was spent in behalf of the
University.

John E. Moore, an experienced itinerant and

directly from the presidency of the Grand Island
district in this Conference, followed to the pastorate
of this charge. He is evidently well equipped,
besides bringing with him a good record as a
preacher and pastor. In him this Church has an
able and trusty manager who will most surely do
good service in all things pertaining to his office.

The Church was not forgetful of the children of
the vicinity, and on the first Sabbath in December,
1890, a Sunday-school was organized with Frank
Johnson as superintendent and A. L. Stonecypher
as asssistant, and four teachers, namely, Mattie
Mason, A. L. Stonecypher, Mrs. F. L. Cotton and
Mary Booth. The attendance on the second Sunday was thirty-nine, and the highest during the
year, fifty-nine. The school met in the hall where
the congregation first worshiped.

In 1891 there was a change in officers, and Mattie Mason was made superintendent. The attendance continued to increase, till in 1892 the average
reached ninety, and the highest number on any one
day was one hundred and ten.

Frank Johnson was again elected superintendent in 1893: and the average attendance for the
year was one hundred and fifteen, and the largest,
one hundred and forty-three.

J. M. Gillan was chosen superintendent in 1894,
and M. W. Ryerson, assistant. The highest
attendance this year was one hundred and forty-
eight, and the school was a center of interest.

During 1895, with Mr. Gillan still at the head, and H. P. Kolb, assistant, the attendance was held at about the same through the cold weather with a prospect of its yet reaching the highest point in its history. The little people are being nurtured and the youths are receiving a training that will be advantageous in after life.

Our people in this Society have grasped the fact that, if a Church shall be perpetuated, the childhood must be trained to take the places of their present instructors.

CHAPTER XIII.

THIS church is located on south Nineteenth and Castellar streets, in the midst of a populous part of the city, though inhabited in a large measure by foreigners. At the time of the organization of the Society it was thought to be a promising movement. Not long afterwards, however, there began to be doubt about the expediency of attempting to keep an organization in existence. The Methodist City Mission and Church Extension Society assumed control, and by the persistence of the presiding elder, T. C. Clendening, the Society was held together, the preaching being done mostly by ministers of the city who had no regular work.

A few men living in the vicinity who were much interested in having a place of worship near at hand, made an efforts to build a church soon after the organization of the Society. Mr. John T. Coatsworth took an active part, and himself being a builder soon accomplished the rearing of a small house which has ever since been used as a chapel. A debt remaining and unpaid was a harassment to the Society during a period when the church was one of the appointments on the Omaha circuit. Bro. Clendening personally obligated himself for money to prevent the property from being sold.

The name of the Society first appears on the
Minutes of the Annual conference in 1891, with
C. B. Allen as pastor.   An attempt was made to
make of it a station, giving the entire time of the
minister to this neighborhood.   Thirty-one members and seventeen probationers were reported as

REV. JOHN P. YOST.

being connected with the charge, and $450 as
contributed towards the pastor's support.   The
property was valued at that time at $2,500.   During
the year Mr. Allen united with another denomination, and George Uhl supplied the charge the
remainder of the year.

In 1892 J. P. Yost was appointed to supply the

work. Only nineteen members could be found at this date, most of whom need not be depended upon for the support of his family. But he and his sanguine wife labored with constancy and in faith, and were rewarded during the winter with an awakening in which about sixty were converted. He reported at the year's end forty-four members and twenty-four probationers, and a Sunday-school of one hundred and eighty-six. Mr. Yost was encouraged so much as to be willing to be returned.

The next year, on account of the beginning of depression in business, many of the people worshiping at Castellar left the city. Twenty-three families took their departure, among them some efficient workers, Sunday-school superintendent, teachers, trustees, etc., very greatly crippling the work. The pastor's support was cut down till he was obliged to use of his private means to subsist.

At the Conference of 1894 it was decided no longer to attempt maintaining this charge by appointing a pastor to serve at his own expense. A Sunday-school, however, was kept up by the assistance of zealous members from other charges in the city.

Several weeks since Dr. Maxfield, the presiding elder, employed J. A. Flowers, a man of good capabilities, to take charge of the work. He has other employment, and spends only the Sabbath with these people, preaching morning and evening but asks nothing of them in the way of compensation. The Sunday-school is doing well, with an attendance of about sixty.

A debt of $600 on the property of the Church is an impediment likely to give trouble, if not the loss of the place of worship. Some philanthropist has presented to him in the case of this Church a good opportunity to spend a little money, which, in a few years, might bring large returns.

CHAPTER XIV.

ONLY a few years since some land was laid out in lots at Benson, about five miles north-west from the Omaha postoffice. Several persons seeking homes outside of the city purchased lots and built residences. A town hall was erected by the land proprietor intended to accommodate public gatherings of the people for all purposes. Soon afterwards a small number of Methodists and others interested in having preaching asked to be included as an appointment on the Omaha circuit. The request was granted; and in June, 1892, J. C. Stewart, a student of the Nebraska Wesleyan University, was given charge of Benson that it might be determined whether such number of people as could give support might be found. But he soon became discouraged and left the field.

The presiding elder, T. C. Clendening, at once employed J. R. Barr to take care of the work till the close of the conference year. Mr. Barr, at the instance of the presiding elder, began agitating the question of building a church, in which direction as much progress was made as to get a promise from Mr. E. A. Benson to donate a lot, when the enterprise was pushed towards further success. He was succeeded by Frederick Tonge in the fall of 1892, who interested himself in the enterprise for a time, but unavoidably failed to consummate the erection of a house. In May, 1893, Articles of Incorporation were written, and the presiding elder called together several citizens and a new Board of Trustees was elected. The old Board was composed of W. P. Coe, Wm. Edge, H. E. McGinnis, J. L. Stewart and Mrs. J. A. Morgan; and the new one included some persons, also, not members of our denomination, and, besides the above, F. Finlayson and Mrs. Coe.

Application was made to the Church Extension Society for a loan of $250, and likewise a donation of an equal sum. The request was granted, on condition of there being secured in subscriptions a certain amount. Owing to the depression already setting in, and, hence, the unwillingness of people to commit themselves for the payment of money, the erection of a building was postponed. Mr. Tonge, however, continued regularly to preach to the congregation till the close of the year.

In the fall of 1893 J. A. Barr for the second time was given charge at Benson, a small missionary appropriation was made to the work, and as he was an unmarried preacher, subsisted at small expense. Services were held weekly at the town hall; a Sunday-school was maintained; and the pastor interested himself in the religious welfare of the young people generally. After the lapse of only a few months Mr. Barr revived the project of a house of worship. Calling the trustees together repeatedly the matter was canvassed and the conclusion was reached that it was possible to effect their purpose. Subscriptions were obtained in sufficient sum to entitle them to the money promised by the Church Extension Society. Through the help and counsel of Dr. Maxfield, the new presiding elder, the promised $500 was obtained in the spring of 1894. The work of construction was begun, and on the Sunday before the meeting of the Annual conference, September 30th, the house was dedicated to the worship of God. Dr. A. Hodgetts preached, and Dr. Maxfield managed the financial business.

The city system of trolley railways extends to Benson, and the location is prized by some who are employed down town as a place of residence on account of cheap lots, rents and fresh air. In a few years it is likely to become even a more desirable suburb for making homes by merchants, mechanics and employees, strengthening, on that account, the little Society already on the ground.

At the last session of the Annual conference, J. Q. A. Flaharty was appointed as Mr. Barr's successor, and is winning friends by his urbane and christian demeanor. His well wrought out sermons as well as the quality of instruction given in the Sunday-school and the League are so helpful that they will be a great blessing to the people of all ages who attend the different services.

The registry of names of officers of the Society at present is as follows:

Rev. J. Q. A. Fleharty, pastor; W. C. Mulford, W. J. Joseph, J. L. Stewart, E. E. Hoffman and Mrs. J. A. Morgan, Trustees; H. M. McGinnis, W. C. Mulford, J. L. Stewart, Mrs. J. A. Morgan and Mrs. Susie Hoffman, Stewards; Frank Wautenpaugh, Sunday-school Superintendent; Frank Hensman, President of Epworth League, and President of Junior League, Miss Mattie Nevins.

CHAPTER XV.

THE question of establishing a Hospital at Omaha had been thought of and discussed by charitable Methodists merely as a necessity, but without any formal or concerted action being taken. The desultory talking had as much effect as to awaken inquiry whether such a movement was practicable, even if all the Methodist Churches in the city would co-operate. Having been agitated to this extent, it was thought best to lay the matter on the hearts of the people, and by that means ascertain if such a project would meet with favor.

The making of a beginning was held in reserve for the time being till the matter might be further investigated. The most inquisitive were on the alert seeking, the while, information. An opportunity came unsought. Mrs. Lucy Rider Meyer, of Chicago, who is reputed as the founder of training schools for nurses in the Methodist Church, accompanied by her husband, on their way to Denver, visited Omaha, and presented to a meeting held in the basement of the First Methodist church some of the features of the work necessary to the organization of a Hospital. This beginning was the occasion of an effort to commence work looking to the establishment of a Hospital and Deaconess Home in this city. The intelligent and satisfactory presentation of the case by these zealous advocates gave inspiration to not a few, and particularly the women present were aroused so thoroughly as to incite them to greater deeds.

Dr. D. A. Foote having lately come to the city from Chicago, whose mother was connected with the training school of that city, was called upon for some statements. He was familiar with the work, and gave some facts corroborating the points made by the others; and which, together, made such an impression as to awaken stirring interest.

The women, by the help and counsel of Mr. B. R. Ball, took up the matter and began operating with a view of securing the help of the pastors and chief laymen of our Church. A committee of men was appointed to formulate the scheme, but brought forth nothing feasible. The pastors took up the subject and tabled a resolution favoring an attempt being made to institute a hospital. The active women became impatient, and at the instance of the Presiding Elder, Rev. T. C. Clendening, presented themselves at the next preachers' meeting and asked that the resolution be taken from the table till they might be heard. Mr. Ball, a staunch advocate and efficient worker, at the request of the women, attended and spoke. Some of the pastors abruptly opposed the undertaking, and all agreed that the time had not yet come to begin such an enterprise. Mr. Clendening, be it said to his credit, unflinchingly favored the women's notion of making a beginning.

The women—Mrs. Haynes, Mrs. Claflin, Mrs. Austin and Mrs. Bryant—pressed the matter with such earnestness and solicitude that the pastors changed their purpose as much as to agree that if $1,500 should be raised as a guarantee of success, they would make no further opposition. Dr. J. W. Shank courageously seconded the presiding elder and the women in an endeavor to make a trial.

In the meantime Dr. Gifford, who was the owner of an Infirmary on South Twentieth, near Harney street, learning of the effort being made, offered the building which he had erected at his own expense, on the condition of an indebtedness of $1,900 being assumed and that there be six rooms reserved for his patients—two for men and two for women—and two besides, subject, however, to the rules of the Hospital. The Hospital Association accepted the proposition, and leasing the ground at $400 a year, opened the institution on May 28th, 1891, for the reception of patients.

Preparatory to this an association was formed, and, to legalize their acts, a Board of Trustees was elected so that property might be conveyed or transferred. The Trustees held their first meeting, Monday, March 2d, 1891, at the rooms of the Young Men's Christian Association building, and organized by electing B. R. Ball, president; J. C.

Cowgill, secretary, and F. W. Hills, treasurer. At this meeting a finance and an executive committee were appointed, and made ready for the transaction of business. On the same day and at the same place the Association met and effected a permanent organization by electing Dr. J. W. Shank, president, and J. C. Cowgill, secretary. A Constitution was adopted, and a committee appointed to secure the legal incorporation of the Association.

The name given the institution is THE METHODIST HOSPITAL and DEACONESS HOME of Omaha. On May 24th, the Hospital and Home was dedicated by Bishop John P. Newman. A preliminary service was held at the First Church, at which time and place Mrs. Claflin read a sprightly paper, and Dr. Crummer a scholarly essay. Bishop Newman's address on "Christianity and Suffering Humanity" was after his usually eloquent style. The statement of B. R. Ball, president of the Trustees, expressing his interest in the movement, had much influence in encouraging the workers to still greater efforts. A large number of people repaired to the Hospital as soon as the services at the church closed where the formal dedication took place.

"The opening of the Hospital," says the *Omaha Christian Advocate*, "is an event of great interest. The Association now owns property worth $10,000, on which there is an indebtedness of $1,900. There has been about $1.500 subscribed for current expenses. The building has capacity for twenty-eight beds."

From the date of the opening till the present a continuous and good work has been done in caring for the sick, maimed and otherwise disabled ones. But the work of caring for such as are admitted to the Hospital cannot be done without expense: and provision had to be made to meet the constantly accumulating outlay. To meet this in part, it was deemed wise to make an inducement for friends and citizens to contribute a small sum by offering an equivalent. Hence, any one in health who may pay into the treasury $10 at one time is entitled to a yearly membership ticket which allows the contributor, in case of personal sickness, to be taken care of without charge, during the year of making the payment.

Receipts from donations of sundry articles for the larder and table, and patients who are able to pay, as well as contributions from all other sources, have been equal to the expenditures. The current expenses are large and increasing, which make the demand for correspondingly larger gifts. The way is open all the while for any benevolence that can be made use of, which will be gratefully received.

The wards and other rooms in the building have been partly furnished without any expense to the Association. For example, Mrs. Claflin furnished four rooms, Mrs. J. W. Nicholson furnished one room, and the Morning Star Mission Band, of Seward Street Church, did likewise. Other parties have provided pieces of appropriate furniture, till the house is furnished so as to keep it running, but still more would be gladly accepted. When the needs of the hospital were first made known, Methodists and others contributed liberally to its assistance. But it became necessary that constant and not spasmodic aid should be secured. Hence, Mrs. Claflin, one of the institution's best friends, and one of the deaconesses spend a good deal of time in traveling, visiting Conferences, and from place to place soliciting help. Some Conferences have agreed to support a bed, individuals have promised to give regularly towards its expenses, and others help when called upon.

The first Board of Trustees was constituted as follows: B. R. Ball, Rev. J. W. Shank, Rev. G. M. Brown, Rev. W. K. Beans, Alex. Hodge, J. E. Cowgill, J. W. Nicholson, S. W. Lindsay, J. J. McLain, L. O. Jones, F. W. Hills, Rev. H. A. Crane, Rev. John Dale, Rev. Alfred Hodgetts and E. M. Richardson.

The first committee appointed to aid in the management was constituted as follows: Mrs. M. A. Claflin, president, and a corps of vice presidents, one from each church in the central part of the city: namely, Mrs. James Haynes, First Church; Mrs. J. J. McLain, Trinity; Mrs. O. J. King, Hanscom Park; Mrs. E. A. Jackson, South Tenth street; Mrs. Hoxie, Seward street; Miss Mattie Mason, Wesley, and Mrs. Harover, Castellar.

In addition to these officers, Miss Alice Pfrimmer serves as Matron and superintendent, with seventeen others constituting the family necessary to take care of the interests of the hospital. These latter include the licensed deaconesses and the number in training for nurses. All of these have either been educated to this work, or are now pursuing the course of study and practice preparatory to receiving license. The force is divided into nursing and visiting deaconesses, some performing duty in the hospital and others visiting families outside, with whom they usually read and pray. Their dress distinguishes them from all other women, and they are recognized by the public as deserving the respect they receive.

Several physicians and surgeons voluntarily devote time and skill to the patients, many of whom are not able to compensate them for their services. And such indigent ones are nursed and fed gratuitously. Those who are able to pay are charged a fee both by the doctors and the hospital.

The facts following, derived chiefly from the Matron, may be of interest to such as are inquiring as to the results of the work. There have been admitted to the Hospital an average of four hundred and fifty patients per year, many of whom are seriously or dangerously sick or injured. Others remain but a short time under treatment and nurs-

ing. The total number cared for since the opening, less than four years ago, is about fifteen hundred. And from September 1st, 1893, till the
same date in 1894, more than $2,000 of free work
has been done!

The management under the superintendence of
Miss Pfrimmer has been economical and satisfactory. But she has been overloaded, having to
make purchases of supplies, direct as to the preparation of food for patients, the distribution of
nurses, and keeping the accounts.

Interest is increasing in respect to a new site
and building for the hospital. A much larger
house is greatly needed and would be quickly filled
by increasing numbers who would apply for privileges and care. If some philanthropists might
be wrought upon to provide the money for such an
enterprise at an early date, a great blessing would
be conferred upon sick and indigent people who
may have no homes of their own nor a pillow on
which to rest their heads.

At the annual meeting of the Association, March
5th, 1895, the following were elected officers for
the ensuing year: Dr. J. B. Maxfield, President:
Rev. W. K. Beans, Vice President; Mr. S. A.
Reynolds, Secretary, and Mr. F. W. White,
Auditor.

The terms of several Trustees having expired,
the following were elected to fill the vacancies:
A. T. Austin, C. W. DeLamatre, H. R. Baldwin,

W. L. Wright, A. S. Cost and Rev. C. N. Dawson: the nine others making a full Board, with J. G. Cortelyou as President.

From the report of the Trustees and Steward the subjoined is obtained:

"To-day, after the hardest year of drought and destitution ever known in this section, and after caring for a daily average of eight free patients, and with delinquent patients bills amounting to nearly $1,600 00, ninety per cent. of which should be considered and really is free work, we come before you practically free of debt, excepting the original purchase money mortgage of $1,900.00.

"Many items contribute to this result. No officer whatever receives any pay. The Deaconesses' faithful work in caring for the internal management; the skillfulness of our medical staff; the free contributions of ice and water, and all kinds of provisions from our friends in the city, in the State and outside the State, have achieved this result."

Mr. W. L. Wright's carefulness as Hospital Steward; Mrs. Claflin's efficient service as Financial Agent, in spite of want of robust health, in securing $756.15; and the skill and success of the medical staff, as evidenced by the low death rate, are appreciatingly spoken of.

It was moved and seconded and carried with enthusiasm that the Board of Trustees proceed to the erection of a new hospital building as soon as feasible.

The report of the Treasurer furnishes the following encouraging facts:

Receipts for the fiscal year 1894 5 ....$8,717.22
Disbursed in the same period......... $.707.41

Leaving a balance on hand of......... $9.81

The building has been kept in good repair and its value now is fully as great as a year ago when it was reported (with contents) at $7,500.00 subject to a mortgage on building of $1,900.00, at 8 per cent   The property is insured for $3,500.00

We have also $1,563.75 of delinquent pay patients' bills due the hospital, but of uncertain value.

The Matron gives the figures showing that a large proportion of the patients treated and nursed up to the date of the meeting were from Omaha and Nebraska.   Out of five hundred and fifty-two received during the year, four hundred and twelve came from our own State.   One hundred and eight from Iowa, and, from other States, only thirty-two.

There were surgical operations performed on three hundred and eighty-five.   The death rate is very small, numbering only nine.

The number in the Hospital family is eighteen. composed of seven deaconesses, and eleven nurses in training, some of whom graduated since the report was made.

CHAPTER XVI.

LIKE all the weekly journals of Methodism, the *Omaha Christian Advocate*, then known by another name, was introduced to the public with very little patronage. The beginning was not significant of success or failure. The preachers were largely depended upon to put it into circulation: and several years of unrequited toil has been part of the experience of its projectors and proprietors.

The making of such a religious newspaper as will win its own way into public favor and secure a widespread reading, requires a constant expenditure of money. The owners or stockholders who have not patience to wait till it shall become self-sustaining might better keep hands off!

The initial denominational weekly of this State took its existence at Hastings, at which place it was published about one year, in the control of Rev. Geo. S. Davis, as editor, and Dr. L. F. Britt as his associate, under the name of the *Nebraska Methodist*. At the instance of friends it was then removed to University Place, from which it was issued two years longer, Geo. S. Davis the while holding the editorial chair.

In 1890, Dr. J. W. Shank purchased an interest in the establishment, with the understanding that the plant should be removed to Omaha, which was shortly afterwards effected, and the first issue of the paper in its new location bears the date of August 9th, 1890. But, on January 1st, following, Mr. Davis disposed of his interest in the business and accepted soon after an appointment as missionary to Bulgaria, leaving the sole ownership in Dr. Shank, who thenceforward conducted both the editorial and business management.

At the session of the General conference at Omaha, May, 1892, Dr. Shank offered the *Advocate* and subscription list as a donation to the publishing agents of the Church, stipulating that the paper should be maintained for four years. The proposal was not accepted, but, instead, a committee consisting of Bishop Newman, Dr. J. W. Shank, Dr. J. B. Maxfield, Rev. John Dale. Dr. C. F. Creighton, B. L. Payne, M. D., Rev. C. A. Mastin, L. H. Rogers and C. F. Weller, Esqs., was appointed to publish, in behalf of the Church, a religious paper in the city of Omaha under the title of the *Omaha Christian Advocate*. The said commission to select an editor subject to the approval of the Book committee, also to conduct the business management of the paper, provided the Church or book committee shall not be in any manner involved in any financial responsibility. The General conference further decreed that, in case of the acceptance of the above conditions, and the publication undertaken in pursuance thereof, it shall be the privilege of any Annual conference or Mission, within convenient access, to adopt the paper as its official organ.

Several weeks subsequent Dr. Shank conceived the idea of organizing a stock company, which was done under and by the authority of the publishing committee. Stock was subscribed, Dr. Shank was elected editor-in-chief, and the *Omaha Christian Advocate* made its appearance under the new regimen, with the first issue of September, 1892; and within one year was adopted by five Annual conferences.

From the date of the removal of the office to Omaha to the end of 1893 the subscription to the paper increased from eight hundred to nearly five thousand.

About the first of January, 1894, an offer was made seeking the purchase of the paper and all its belongings. A sale was soon consummated, and on January 15th Dr. Shank resigned, and Rev. Frank Crane was elected editor by the commission. The form of the paper was changed from that of eight pages to sixteen, but much reduced in size of fold, and a new and better dress was put on.

The improved appearance was much prized by readers; and the matter with which its columns were filled was enticing.

After conducting the paper six months, with J. G. Cortelyou as business manager and Major E. W. Halford as an editorial contributor, Mr.

Crane, in the meantime having the care of a Church with a numerous membership, and great interests pending, found that he was overloaded. Taking the counsel of friends, a proposition was made to Dr. Shank and accepted, taking the editorship and control of the *Advocate* off his hands.

Dr. Shank again assumed the responsibility, and after being fairly installed issued the first number under the new management, July 28th, 1894. It was set in new type and wore a comely head. The name of J. W. Shank, D. D., stands over the editorial column, and that of his son, W. W. Shank, as associate. And E. W. Halford is continued as editorial contributor.

Of the Methodist institutions of the city the *Advocate* is not the least, and has already become a factor in helping to build up the cause of Christianity, by giving assistance to the pastors and educating its readers. And, with increasing circulation, will become a desideratum throughout its patronizing territory. The demand in other States for local religious papers, through the columns of which the early publication of special and other important notices may be secured, rather than sending them abroad, is meeting with favor.

A home paper is of use as a vehicle of communication by which any local news may be placed before the eyes of its readers before it is out of date. And personals, letters and articles discussing matters of local interest to the territory embraced in its field, which might be regarded as void of pertinency by the older Church organs would be relished by its readers, intensifying the necessity for its existence.

The question hitherto unsettled and debatable, whether local Church papers can be maintained, is nearly solved. But in the solution a good deal of patronage has been taken from the larger organs, while many more households read the local papers.

CHAPTER XVII.

THE personage whose name heads this chapter
has been prominently before the Church since
1860.   He was first recognized as a student, trav-
eler and author, laborious, thorough and practical;
and now at the age of sixty-eight still takes pleasure in study and travel, and wields a pen with
facility and of extraordinary correctness and power.

The Bishop is never unemployed, but is all the
while busy either with his episcopal duties directly,
or in preaching for some pastor, lecturing, in transit
to some point where needed, or aiding in some
church or college enterprise both with speech and
money.   His correspondence by letter is immense,
taking his time when at home to an extent that
forbids any leisure.   But, nevertheless, he seldom
goes before an audience without ample preparation, and is always heard with interest from the
pulpit or platform on any topic he enunciates or
theme he discloses, invariably calling out large
congregations.   Rev. Dr. Maxfield pronounces
him the Daniel Webster of the American Methodist pulpit.

His studious habits and wide range of reading
and travel in earlier and later life provide him
abundantly with resources upon which he can

depend when needed for any great or appropriate occasion. His rugged and nearly unimpaired physical health enables him to endure fatigue and application with very little weariness, and intellectual exercise in a search after truth, when not over-worked, furnishes him with extreme pleasure.

When at home in Omaha, where his official residence has been for seven years, though covetous of hours, and enough on hand besides to engage every minute of daylight, he takes time to be respectful to clergymen who call upon him for advice or information. He seems to participate in the success of gifted and devoted men and partakes of the good cheer of capable pastors, but can hardly tolerate thriftless and sluggish preachers who fail of bringing about results commensurate with their opportunities.

The Bishop's personal appearance and dignified bearing impress friends, observers and strangers that there belongs to him the qualities worthy of the office he ably fills. His well-knit, stout frame as he stands erect in the pulpit, or his supple movements in making calls on foot, augurs years of steady, unflagging usefulness to the Church and the world.

The following biographical sketch is chiefly obtained from other sources:

"John P. Newman, D. D., LL. D., was born in the city of New York, September 1st, 1826, and at the age of sixteen was converted and united with

the Methodist Episcopal Church. He acquired an
academic education at Cazenovia Seminary in his
native State. At twenty-two he entered the traveling connection in the Oneida Conference. Seven

BISHOP JOHN P. NEWMAN, D. D.

years later he was transferred to the Troy Conference and appointed successively to Amsterdam,
Albany, and Bedford street, New York City.

Going abroad in 1859 he traveled through

Europe, spending a winter in Rome, as student, and thence making a tour of Egypt and Palestine, writing letters to *The Methodist* which received the highest commendation. On his return Harper Brothers published his work " From Dan to Beersheba," which is regarded as an authority by biblical students. In 1862-3 he was pastor of the Washington Square Church, New York city. At the instance of Bishop Ames he was then sent in war times to reorganize the old Church in Louisiana, Mississippi and Texas. He founded a University and established the *South Western Christian Advocate* at New Orleans. His services in this field were of great benefit to the Church and National government. General Sheridan having command of the Crescent City, and the military district surrounding, almost daily called him into counsel.

In 1869 he was appointed pastor of the Metropolitan Church at Washington, D. C., the costliest edifice for worship belonging to American Methodism, the Society of which he organized; and while serving this Church was for three terms Chaplain of the United States Senate. Under the appointment of President Grant, in 1873, he made the tour of the world. His commercial reports, made from observation, were the best the government ever received. On his return he was re-appointed to the Metropolitan Church. In 1877 he was transferred to the New York Conference and served

Central Methodist Church in New York City three years, succeeding some of the denomination's greatest pulpit orators.

As a result of his protracted tour abroad in 1859 and 1860, the Harpers published for him his work entitled "Babylon and Nineveh," which secured for him membership in the Archæological Society of London. In 1881 he was appointed by the Bishops a member of the Ecumenical Conference, which met in London, before which he read a valuable paper.

Returning from England he located that he might produce certain literary works on foreign travel. In 1885 he was readmitted to the New York Conference with unanimity and demonstrations of esteem, from which he was transferred to the Baltimore Conference, and again stationed at the Metropolitan Church at Washington."

Four years ago, in taking his share of the travel and duties of the episcopacy, he crossed the Pacific to visit our Mission in Japan; and the year following he made an episcopal tour to our South American Missions, visiting both the western and eastern coasts, as well as making flying trips interiorward. Last year he was allotted the superintendence of our European Missions, and visited Italy, Bulgaria, Prussia, Sweden, Norway and Finland, consuming the entire summer.

Dr. Newman, as he was known before his election to the episcopacy, filled the pastorate of the

Metropolitan Church nine years, and during the presidency of General Grant an enduring intimacy was encouraged between the chief magistrate and the eminent divine that continued to the close of the chieftain's life. This friendship brought him into contact with public men and national affairs, extending his influence to his individual advantage. In 1884 he made the transit of the continent, at the request of California's senator, to deliver a funeral oration on Leland Stanford, jr., and afterwards performed the same office in respect to Generals Grant and Logan.

He received the degree of Doctor of Divinity from a university at Rochester, New York, when he was thirty-eight years of age, and the degree of Doctor of Laws from the Grant Memorial University, of Athens, Tennessee. The Bishop is author also of "Christianity Triumphant" and "Evenings with the Prophets on the Lost Empire of the World." Since his residence in Omaha he published a work on the "Supremacy of Law." He was elected Bishop in 1888, since which date he has, without intermission, given his time and strength to the performance of the duties of the great office.

CHAPTER XVIII.

REV. W. E. SLAUGHTER, D.D.

THE Church is indebted to some men more than others. Those who can do the work of the ministry with facility and, at the same time, efficiently are certain to be recognized by their superiors and fellow-workers as worthy of place and authority. Such indications of usefulness are seldom overlooked, and reward is sure to follow.

The culture of the subject of this sketch at the outset of his ministerial life and during the days of his greatest activity, was above that of a large majority of the preachers of our Church, hence, his calls to conspicuous appointments and some-times to remote fields. Fidelity to his convictions would not tolerate any resistance to authority coming from the episcopacy, though obedience might be at great personal sacrifice.

Mr. Slaughter's first pastoral work was at Palmyra, New York; his second field, Carlton, and so on. Later he was stationed at Niagara street, Buffalo. Through the persuasion of friends he left the more active work of the ministry and accepted the principalship of an academy in Pennsylvania, and later that of the Genesee Model School, Lima, N. Y. A few years after, removing to the West, he became a member of the Rock River Conference and was appointed to Wabash avenue, Chicago, in which charge he served a full term: thence Joliet, and afterwards Rockford.

Early during the late rebellion he raised a company of volunteers for the 39th Illinois infantry, expecting to be appointed chaplain of the regiment. But the men whom he recruited insisted upon his being their captain, to whose preference he yielded. However he actually served as chaplain, organizing class and prayer meetings and seeking the conversion of soldiers. Serving twenty-one months, toiling with heroic zeal, he was disabled and returned to his family. Recovering as nearly as to permit him to perform pastoral work, he was appointed to Rockford, Illinois.

In the midst of his labors at Rockford, in the spring of 1864, Bishop Ames sought him as the man he wanted for Denver district, Colorado. The matter was urged, and he finally consented. The people whom he was serving remonstrated, and telegraphed the Bishop asking that he might not be removed. But the reply came—"He must go." He left at once and hurriedly, only delaying long enough to provide a private conveyance that his family might follow. He reached the seat of the Colorado Conference just in time to hear the appointments read at the close of the session, and was startled to hear his own name announced for Colorado district instead of Denver.

The last-named district, at that date, included

all of the southern part of the territory and was made up of a few preaching places a great distance apart, the largest of which was Colorado City, once the capital, having less than ten members. The sacrifice he must make was unexpected, but there was no loyal way out of it. Heroically he accepted the work and sent for his wife and two sons, leaving his daughter that she might attend school. There was no railway reaching further west than Marshalltown, Iowa. Mrs. Slaughter sent her eldest, a boy of seventeen, with the conveyance for crossing the plains in advance, and, taking the rail, overtook him at the western terminus. They together hence began the long and hazardous journey, expecting to meet bands of Indians after crossing the Missouri river.

Arriving at Omaha they were kindly received by Rev. T. B. Lemon, pastor, and his family, who persuaded them to rest a few days. Mrs. S. says: "I started from Omaha with my two boys, the older serving as driver, and the other two years old, feeling there was safety only in the protection of the divine arm." Often their vehicle was surrounded by the red men, who, at that time, were committing frequent depredations, but they were not molested. Four weeks of wearisome travel had passed, and an axle of their carriage broke when several miles from any habitation, and they were helplessly alone. Fortunately a covered wagon came in sight. They were taken on board, and their conveyance was drawn behind; and in this manner were driven into Denver where they were met by Mr. S.

Tarrying long enough to get the carriage repaired, the trip toward Pike's Peak was resumed. Colorado City being their destination. Their arrival was in the evening, only to find that there was but one place where they could get lodging for the night; and but one frame house in the village: the others were of logs. They could make no arrangement for housekeeping, and could find no place where they could all occupy the same house—they had to be separated for sleeping. As their money was nearly gone, Mrs. S. began teaching, while her husband made a round on the district, taking about a month.

Mr. Slaughter attempted to make better provision for his family's comfort. In his travels he found some mineral springs, and as he had never used his right to Government land he concluded to claim them as a homestead. Upon this claim he and his son put up a log house, and while yet unfinished the family occupied it. Retiring the first night while the stars could be seen through the undaubed apertures and the air balmy and quiet, an unlooked for change in the temperature occurred before morning. The wind blew cold and biting and snow began flying; and daylight found Mr. S. with a severe cold that soon developed in pneumonia. He summoned a doctor who invited him to his cabin, one room of which he occupied for two months. By the watchful care of the physician he was brought through the crisis. But the doctor advised that he would convalesce more surely in the altitude of Denver.

Mrs. S. says: "Our finances were meager, and living very costly. When we broke our last dollar it indeed looked very dark ahead. But I felt surely the Lord will provide. And he did; for the next mail brought a check for $50 from Gov. Evans who had heard of Mr. Slaughter's illness. This enabled us to outfit for Denver."

The carriage and team of mules had been kept, and the family at once quit the scenes of suffering and privation, and likewise their homestead on which stands now the thriving city of Colorado Springs. They arranged to start on Monday. A snow storm began on Sunday, but Mr. S., feeble as he was, insisted on pulling out the next day, though the wind blew the snow furiously. A bed was made in the wagon to afford as much comfort as possible to the now emaciated presiding elder. Encountering the first snow drift the team refused to go through; and when urged, lay down, and had to be stripped of their harness to get them on their feet. The only means of making headway required that Mrs. S. and the boy Bradner should tramp a path in advance of their obstinate team. In this manner they managed to travel ten miles that day, and in the evening put up at the "Dirty Woman's

ranch." The next day, by the same means, a fif-
teen-mile drive was made, and at dusk reached a
ranch kept by a Methodist woman. A cheery welcome was given, and a meal prepared the like of
which they had not partaken of for months!

Later in the evening a government team of six
mules was driven up drawing a great wagon in
which were several soldiers. In the morning the
soldiers proposed that Mr. S and his wife should
be transferred to their wagon, in which manner
they were taken to Denver. After spending several weeks at the City of the Plains and receiving
no benefit, his physician suggested that Mr. S.
must return to the States. Their friends at Rockford, Illinois, having learned of their troubles
remitted $150, by the using of which they made
their way to Chicago.

Mr. Slaughter was brought across the plains on
a bed in a freight wagon. The trip was one of
fatigue and anxiety to his wife. From a robust
man of two hundred and ten pounds he had been
reduced to one hundred and thirty-two; and for
many months after returning his recovery was
doubtful.

His devoted wife with ceaseless solicitude
attended her husband on this tedious overland
journey, for which she received grateful mention
from their many friends. And her helpful, intelligent and willing efforts thereafter, and as long as
he lived, in bearing her share of the burdensome

sacrifices in the ministry as an itinerant's wife, should be recorded as a perpetual example. Nor was she ready to relinquish her toil after her husband had gone to rest. Her younger son must be educated at a denominational school outside of the State. Using her preserved energy she accomplished her purpose, and now enjoys the result of her interest in his welfare in seeing him ordained and installed in the work of the ministry.

As soon as Mr. Slaughter's health allowed he re-entered the effective work. Meanwhile he made a trip to Nebraska City to help establish his eldest son in business. By request he preached, and among the auditors was a Methodist from Omaha, who, on reaching home, spoke so favorably of the sermon, that a telegram was sent asking him to come and preach on the next Sabbath. He responded by his presence, preached, and was waited upon and invited to accept the pastorate of the Church. Consenting, he entered upon his first work in Nebraska, in which State he remained ever after till his death, which occurred at his home in the suburbs of Omaha, July 26th, 1879.

Mr. S.'s introduction to Omaha, and his invitation to accept the pastorate of the Church, was for the purpose of filling out a fraction of a year. The pulpit had been left vacant by the dismissal of W. M. Smith in 1865; and the following two years he served very acceptably receiving each year a salary of $1,500. At the session of the Conference

at Peru, April, 1868, he was granted a supernumerary relation. In 1870 he was again made
effective and appointed to Bellevue, where he
remained two years: in 1872-3, Brownville: in 1874-
5 and 6, Lincoln, when he was appointed to the
Omaha district, in 1877. During the second year
in the office of presiding elder he ceased at once to
work and live, at the age of fifty-six years.

While stationed at Brownville he wrote an able
work entitled "Modern Genesis," which he published in 1876. At the time of his death he had
collected a good deal of matter for, and com-
menced writing, a history of Methodism in
Nebraska. He was an able and frequent corre-
spondent of our Church periodicals, a careful
student and an accurate thinker; and if his life
had been spared longer the Church would have
derived more substantial evidence of his worth.

William B. Slaughter was born near Pen Yann,
Yates county, N. Y., July 15th, 1823. In his
youth he yearned for an education. His father,
though an intelligent farmer, was not inclined to
favor his son's ambition. His privileges were
limited to attending a country school only during
the winter season. In the cropping and harvest-
ing seasons his services were required on the farm.
Sometimes while at work in the field he managed
to keep a book before him by attaching a small
frame to the handle of the plow, and in this way
solved problems or conjugated latin verbs.

His father perceiving his longing for more knowledge reluctantly consented to his going from home to attend a school of higher grade. But he had to begin teaching at the age of sixteen to provide means with which to pay expenses, and could attend school only the remainder of the time. By practicing the strictest economy he enabled himself finally to enter Genesee College, at which he took a thorough course. as a classmate of Wm. H. DePuy, who afterwards and for a long time was assistant editor of *The Christian Advocate*, and through the columns of the great paper made extensive and appreciative mention of his death.

Mr. Slaughter received the degree of D. D. from Allegheny College, and did honor to the distinction in after life. At the General conference held at Baltimore, in 1876, Dr. Slaughter was chairman of the delegation elected by his Conference. He was also appointed by the General conference a member of the Book Committee to assist in scanning the work and accounts of the agents of the Book Concern.

CHAPTER XIX.

DR. T. B. LEMON was born in Charlestown. Virginia, November 3d, 1819, and at the date of his demise was in his seventy-first year. His death occurred at his home in Omaha, surrounded by his family, at 10 o'clock Wednesday night, February 19th, 1890, after an illness of only a few weeks. He had been indisposed, however, for several months on account of aggravating pulmonary trouble affecting mostly his throat; but later assuming a more serious character, prostrated him, and to which his vital forces had to succumb. It is needless to say that his decease was the occasion for mourning throughout the State because a good and useful man and friend had fallen.

He left the wife of his younger years and five grown up children—three sons and two daughters —all of whom, except the eldest son, live in Omaha. If he had lived one day longer the forty-fourth anniversary of his married life would have occurred.

No Methodist preacher was more widely known in Nebraska than Thos. B. Lemon. His labors were intimately connected with the history of the denomination in this State for thirty years, and had been distributed nearly over all portions of the growing commonwealth.

Dr. Lemon entered upon the work of the ministry in the old Baltimore Conference, where he labored for ten years, often preaching to mixed congregations of whites and slaves, the latter admiring him much as the former. For reasons of his own he desisted, and, turning his attention to the law, removed to Chicago. Afterwards, in 1857, he sought a new field in the farther west. Settling in Bellevue, Nebraska Territory, he opened a law and land office. But before the end of three years he decided to re-enter the ministry, and accepted work under the presiding elder of the Omaha district, John M. Chivington. He was given charge, in 1860, of De Soto, at that time an important steamboat landing south of the present site of Blair.

In the spring of 1861 the Kansas-Nebraska Conference was divided, the latter henceforward including only the Territory of Nebraska. The session was held at Nebraska City, and he was admitted and appointed to the city in which the conference was held, at that date the best and most populous town in the Territory, where he labored for two years. At the close of this term he was appointed to Omaha City, Isaac Burns being presiding elder. In 1865 Mr. Lemon was himself elevated to the office of presiding elder and appointed to Omaha district, which at that time comprised all the settled territory in the State north of the Platte river,. Long and tedious drives over unworked roads, poor accommodations for himself and team were part of the lot of the incumbent of the office.

Closing his term on this district, in 1869, he was transferred to Nebraska City district. Till this date there had been but two districts in the conference; but settlements began being made up the Platte and to the west so rapidly that a new map of the country was needing, and a third district was constructed, which, in honor of America's great president, was christened Lincoln. After two years of labor on the Nebraska City district, he was appointed the second time to Nebraska City station, where he remained three years, the limit of the pastoral term having been extended.

Dr. Lemon was returned to Omaha in the fall of 1874 and stationed at the Eighteenth Street Church, which had hitherto been known as Second Church, and located at Izard and Twenty-first street. The building was moved during the summer from the old to the new location and fitted up in tasteful style. The Society was made up in part of the persons who felt they could no longer tolerate the action of the officers of the First Church, and others who had a membership in the Second Church before the house was moved to the new site. He served these people one year, when his capabilities as the president of a district could no longer be dispensed with, and he was returned to Nebraska City district to fill out the term.

At the session of the Conference at Omaha, in 1877, Mr. Lemon was appointed by Bishop Bowman as presiding elder of Kearney district on the western margin of population. This region had been almost devastated by grasshoppers only two years before. It included at that time all there was of western Nebraska beyond Kearney. With some reluctance he took charge of this pioneer field, but courageously entered upon the execution of duty as an obedient Methodist clergyman, though dubious that his strength was adequate to the task before him.

The first two years it kept the name of Kearney district. The following four years, the work having expanded, it was known as West Nebraska Mission, and Mr. Lemon was made by the bishops, superintendent. At the expiration of the sixth year the territory was organized as an Annual conference, and he was appointed again presiding elder of Kearney district, which now in territory was small compared with itself six years before.

But the hard work and exposure had worn greatly upon him. Soon after Conference he and his devoted wife went to Denver in order to give him some relief from work and a little time to recuperate before entering upon his duties on the district. After returning he started to North Platte to hold a quarterly meeting. While in transit he was smitten with paralysis on the train and had to be taken home. The following Febru-

ary he was seized with a second stroke. Recovering as much as to be able to travel he sought
vigor in California. Keeping charge of the district till the close of the year, he was given the
appointment of Tract agent merely to save him
from superannuating; and at the ending of the
second year was transferred, first to the Nebraska
Conference, and was made financial agent of the
Wesleyan University, at Lincoln. In a short
time, preferring to have his home at Omaha, he
was transferred to the North Nebraska Conference.
He was holding the office of agent at his death.

After going to the immense district to which he
was unexpectedly appointed—a district comprising
20,000 square miles, including thirty counties, the
larger share of which had to be organized for
church work—Mr. Lemon visited Ogalalla. Here
he found only cattle owners and herders, who, on
his proposing to preach to them, made an arrangement for services by procuring a place and making
known to their comrades that there would be
preaching at a certain hour. A good-sized assembly met to whom he discoursed in a manner that
satisfied them that they had heard no ordinary
man. At the close, a suggestion was made by
some one of the audience that a collection be
taken; and in a few minutes $75 were secured and
handed to him, besides their paying his hotel bill.
He was besought to return and hold service
again.

The above notes are indicative of the esteem in which Mr. Lemon was held by the people among whom and in whose interests he labored. His judicious and hearty familiarity with his friends, whether in or out of the Church, was never challenged. His personnel was impressive; though possessing a stalwart frame, his kind and benignant face was an index that no one need feel afraid of his approach. The welcome he would give his friends would insure from them reciprocal kindness. No Methodist preacher living in Omaha ever acquired among the chief citizens more reverence than he.

Rev. Dr. Maxfield, an intimate and old associate in the Conference, in speaking him, says: "My acquaintance with Dr. Lemon dates back to 1861, the year of the admission of both of us to the traveling ministry. He has always exercised a commanding influence in the Church. In his prime he was counted among its foremost orators. In later years he was characterized by prudence, sound judgment and far-seeing sagacity. He was a faithful servant of the Church and of his family. His friendship was true as the needle to the pole. He will not be forgotten nor his place soon be filled."

Nor is this all of Dr. Lemon's history. His superiors in authority appointed him a member of the general Missionary committee in which office he served four years, and a like term as a member

of Church Extension committee. He was elected
by the ministerial members of the Conference
which he served as a delegate to the General conference, twice. First to the session which met in
Brooklyn, N. Y., in 1872; and next in Cincinnati,
in 1880.

As a preacher, Dr. Lemon was argumentative
and didactic, always purposing to give his hearers
something instructive and helpful. He was, in a
word, a teacher of the Word, and eloquently
impressed his thoughts upon his auditors. His
sermons were convincing and well elucidated. In
the earlier days of Methodism in Nebraska he
deserved and received the chief appointments,
where his influence in the pulpit and in pastoral
work might be most efficient.

CHAPTER XX

REV. John B. Maxfield, D. D., was born at Syracuse, N. Y., in 1832; and was converted in a revival held by the Wesleyan Methodists at Waddell's meeting house, Knox County, Ohio, February, 1856. Soon after this he left Ohio, and early sought a membership in the Methodist Episcopal Church at Waymansville, Indiana, in April, 1856. Going to Kansas the following year he was just in time to familiarize himself with the contention as to whether that Territory should be free or slave soil.

Thenceforward regarding himself called to preach the gospel, he was recommended by the proper body and admitted on trial at the first session of the Nebraska Annual conference holding at Nebraska City, April, 1861, Bishop Morris presiding. From that date to the present his membership has been continuous. He prides himself in never having missed the roll-call at the opening of a session. The entire settled portions of the Territory of Nebraska were included in the Conference at the time of his admission. Twenty-two preachers were appointed to fields of labor, and the lay membership reported to be 948.

Mr. Maxfield's first appointment was to

Beatrice circuit as junior, Joel Mason being his colleague and preacher in charge; and in 1862 he had charge of De Soto; 1863, Decatur, from which circuit, after making one round, he was removed by the presiding elder, Isaac Burns, to take the superintendency of the Pawnee Manual Labor school, where he remained four years; 1867-8, Bellevue; 1869, Mt. Pleasant; 1870, Plattsmouth: 1871, presiding elder of Beatrice district, serving a full term of four years; and at the expiration of the term was transferred, in 1875, to the North Nebraska district, serving which four years, he was appointed at the nineteenth session of the Conference, held at Lincoln, October, 1879, to First Church, Omaha. After serving two years, though his Official Board requested his return, Bishop Foster, partly on account of the Conference territory having been divided, overruled his personal protest and appointed him to the Omaha district, which he served the following four years. In 1885 Bishop Andrews appointed, him at the request of the Trustees of that institution, to the presidency of the North Nebraska Conference College, at Central City. At the end of eighteen months ill health compelled his resignation. Taking a trip to California and the resting from application to study, his health was in a measure restored by the meeting of the next session of Conference, and he was appointed to the Norfolk district, which he served the full limit of six years.

The writer, in the columns of one of our official papers, said of him when his work was nearly closed on the last-named district: Dr. Maxfield is closing his term on the district most satisfactorily to himself and his preachers. He has been able to meet every appointment during the past year, and his health is now more rugged than formerly. The Doctor has good gifts for filling the office, and, by the way, has a happy facility in helping the preachers who are in his care. He has an eye to every kind of church work, and lends aid to every enterprise that may be on hand which promises to promote the cause of God or be of avail in any manner to the membership. His plans are usually well-contrived and he executes them without friction."

He was again appointed to the Omaha district at the session of Conference at Norfolk, September, 1893, after the boundary of the district had been narrowed on the north and west.

Dr. Maxfield was elected by his ministerial brethren four times as delegate to the General conference—Brooklyn, Philadelphia, New York and Omaha sessions. And he served one quadrennium as a member of the General Missionary and Church Extension committees. He was foremost in 1884 in settling the boundary line between the North Nebraska and West Nebraska Conferences, advocating and assuring the change before the committee on boundaries in the General conference.

He took an active part in 1888 in securing the following session of the General conference at Omaha; and was appointed at that session one of the seven commissioners to fix upon the place of holding the session of 1892.

Dr. Maxfield is widely known in this State, first as a circuit rider pioneering in new settlements, and later as sharing with his co-workers in the best appointments, as well as receiving honors from the Church and his peers. But he has spent more than half of his life in the ministry in traveling districts, for which work, in the judgment of the bishops, he has skillful adaptation. His long and unremitting labors in Nebraska entitle him to be recognized as the senior and patron of the Conference. His acquaintance with many of the leading men of the denomination, and his intimacy with several of the bishops, give him an enviable prestige which he aims to use to no one's hurt. In the Conference his influence is unimpaired and legitimate.

No one in the Conference is invited oftener to dedicate churches. In this work he is popular as a money-getter, and on account of his personal liberality in assisting, if need be, with his own check on the bank. His contributions are noteworthy because of their frequency, and his willingness to assist in every enterprise the Church in his field has projected.

As a preacher he is lucid, versatile and extemporaneous, speaking as one having authority to promulgate the doctrines of the christian life, and to represent the theology of the Church in whose ministry he is a mouthpiece. He enjoys the privilege of the pulpit, and uses it as a forum from which to plead the cause he advocates; and with fluent and ornate speech, pure diction and thoughtful logic to demonstrate the profit there is in godliness. Though seldom using a manuscript in discoursing, his sermons read as if their composition had been well matured, and are ingeniously arranged.

In debate on the conference floor, when aroused, his declamation is earnest and incisive, but rarely vindictive.

Presiding in Quarterly conference Dr. Maxfield appears to as good advantage as in the discharge of any of the duties of his office. He prepares himself for the work to be done in the chair, and is able to instruct in Church or parliamentary law; and his rulings are rarely ever questioned, or an appeal taken from his decisions.

An occurrence of no ordinary kind while Dr. Maxfield was an Omaha pastor, in 1880, is given here as a bit of history: When General Grant took a brief lay-off at Omaha, on his memorable trip around the world, in answer to an invitation from the pastor, the ex-president attended service at the First Methodist Episcopal Church, on Sunday, and was an interested listener from the pew

to one of Dr. Maxfield's best discourses. The
event was heralded to the world by newspaper
reporters who came from abroad and were favored
with admission to the sanctuary.

While living in Kansas he was one day traversing a prairie on horseback when two armed bush-
whackers rode up one on each side of him, and at
the point of revolvers, captured him. He was
unarmed, and for a few minutes felt more than
uncomfortable. He was suspected, and correctly,
too, of being in sentiment with the free state movement at that time causing a bitter and uncompro-
mising hostility from the advocates of more slave
territory. In a few minutes, and before a decision
was reached in respect to his case, there came in
sight two footmen. His captors probably thinking
two captives better than one, left young Maxfield
that they might quickly investigate the rights of
the others. But Mr. Maxfield made use of his
chance by putting spurs to his horse, and turning
aside from the trail, made good time at right angles
from the course he had been traveling, and escaped.
This little episode clings vividly to his recollection
yet as being a purposed providential interference.
God had a work for him to do in His vineyard.

During Dr. Maxfield's term of service on the
North Nebraska district he came very nearly being
drowned in a swollen and unbridged stream that he
attempted to ford in the night. He and two gentlemen riding in a spring wagon drawn by a pair of

fine horses started to a quarterly meeting eighteen miles distant, and late in the afternoon encountered a terrific rain and thunder storm. They were soon thoroughly drenched, but a majority decided to continue the journey till reaching their destination. About three miles short of the place they came to a creek so full of water that almost as soon as the horses stepped in they began swimming. The darkness was intense. The team in swimming was washed by the surging current below the exit, facing an abrupt bank. The horses turned down the stream, the wagon upset in, perhaps, ten feet of water with the presiding elder under it. He was under the water and on the surface alternately till almost exhausted, and at last began swimming down stream in search of a landing place. Finding a clump of weeds, he felt for and found the bottom. His companions had reached the bank and came to his relief. The horses were drowned, he lost his satchel filled with his manuscript sermons, books and clean linen, and had no dry suit in which to appear either in private or public.

CHAPTER XXI.

REV. HENRY T. DAVIS.

THE person and character mentioned is well known in central and southern Nebraska as a pioneer Methodist preacher. He has filled so many fields of labor to which his itinerary has called him during more than thirty-five years of continuous traveling as a circuit rider, stationed pastor and presiding elder that he knows nearly every appointment in the region designated.

At the period of his landing in Nebraska there were no charges that could offer the inducement of a good salary to a preacher. Mr. Davis had to take the risk, and depend for sustenance on the generosity of the people whom he served. If his support was meagre, but at the same time, a willingness to contribute to his living was shown, he would do with less, however much he might be pinched for the commonest of food and clothing. He is well qualified to furnish facts and figures respecting an itenerant's life and sacrifices in early times in Nebraska. Many of such facts and some of the figures are given in his book, "Solitary Places Made Glad," which he published a few years since. He passed through the roughing era, and is at this day able to perform duty cheerfully and effectively on the Beatrice district in the Nebraska Conference.

As a presiding elder he has spent more than one-third of his time since coming west, and bids fair to be able to work for years to come.

Henry T. Davis was born in Springfield, Ohio, July 29th, 1832, and was converted March 4th, 1853, at South Bend, Indiana. He was inclined to the ministry from the beginning of his religious life; and soon after his conversion a friend provided him with a scholarship at Asbury (now De Pauw) University. Before the expiration of his probationary membership in the Church, he was appointed class leader by the pastor at Greencastle, the seat of the University. On the 23d of June, 1855, he was examined on "Doctrines and Discipline" by the presiding elder, Aaron Wood, before the Quarterly conference, and the next morning license to preach was put in his possession.

Mr. Davis was admitted on trial in the Northwest Indiana Conference and ordained deacon by Bishop Waugh, in October, 1857, and appointed to Russellville circuit as junior preacher. The following two years he was sent to Sanford circuit as preacher in charge. In the summer of 1858 and in the midst of a prosperous year he had such a desire to go west that he resigned his charge, packed and shipped his household effects to a new destination. This removal was hastened by the receipt of a letter from his half-brother, Wm. M Smith, at that time pastor of our Church at Omaha, at which point he landed from a Missouri river steamer, July 13th, and supped at Col. John Richie's that evening. Bellevue circuit had been reserved for him by the presiding elder, Wm. H. Goode, and he soon afterwards took charge of the uncultivated field.

He shall be permitted to tell the story of his introduction to Bellevue circuit in his own way: "When we reached Bellevue we found no Church organization. The outlook was not encouraging, but gloomy in the extreme. A class had been organized but had gone down. Methodism had no standing. and the people looked at us with curious eyes. The foundation of the Church had to be laid, and we were there for that purpose, and went to work with a will. I sent an appointment to preach at Fairview eight miles west, and on Sunday morning started on horseback. We had been told that it was beautifully located, overlooking all the surrounding country. I rode on till I thought it must be near, and began looking for the new town. At length, away to the right of the road. I saw a little shanty; reined up my horse, and turned towards the shanty, but before reaching it was met by the man of the house. I said, 'Will you tell me the way to Fairview?'

"'O, yes: which way did you come?'

"'From Bellevue.'

"'You came the traveled road, I suppose?'

"'Yes, sir.'

··· You passed Fairview two miles east of this. There are no houses there yet !'

"I told him I had sent an appointment to preach there that day.

··· Go back. Robert Laing lives there, and I expect the meeting is to be at his house.' I rode back, saw a log cabin off to the south, with some trees about it, and found a number of people waiting for the preacher. In a grove near by I preached my first sermon in Nebraska to about a dozen hearers."

Remaining in charge of the circuit till the end of the conference year, in the meantime having moved to a claim eight miles west of Bellevue, Mr. Davis attended the meeting of the Conference in April, 1859, at Omaha. He was admitted by transfer, and on the Sabbath ordained elder by Bishop Scott. From the Bishop he received, at this session, his appointment to Omaha.

In speaking of the removal from the claim to his new charge, Mr. Davis says:

"To obtain a carriage in which to ride was out of the question. We tried to hire a span of horses and wagon in which to move, but in vain. So we had to do the next best thing, take what we could get—an ox team. Into the wagon we loaded our goods, and about the twenty-fifth day of April the pastor of the Methodist Episcopal Church of Omaha, and his wife, might have been seen riding behind a yoke of oxen up Farnam street and down Seventeenth to the parsonage."

At the fourth session of the Kansas-Nebraska Conference, which met at Omaha April 14th, 1859, Mr. Davis was first introduced to his co-laborers in the ministry, and henceforth shared with his brethren in enduring or enjoying, as the case might be, whatever fell to his lot in regard to fields of labor. Before he had been three years on Nebraska soil he was appointed in April, 1861. presiding elder of Nebraska City district. The area of the district included all of the charges south of the Platte river, covering the territory of the present Nebraska Conference and the eastern part of the West Nebraska.

Mr. Davis has served as presiding elder two terms on the Nebraska City district, one term on the Lincoln district, part of a term on the Omaha district and is now serving on Beatrice district. He has twice been a delegate from his own Conference to the General conference, first in 1864, and again in 1876.

His exposures have been enough to wear a man out, but through all he escaped nearly unharmed. He now preaches with earnestness and effect, and has been the means of leading a great many to Christ during the long term of years he has faithfully spent in the vineyard of the Lord.

CHAPTER XXII.

GEO. W. FROST was the son of a Methodist preacher: his birthplace being in New England amid the rugged scenery of the Green Mountain State, at Barre, Vermont. His father willingly subjecting himself to all the privations of the life of an itinerant, at any early day moved to the vicinity of Boston. Like other traveling preachers, however, of that period in the history of the denomination, his stay was limited to one, or at most, two years in the same charge. But the education of his children was attended to with the utmost care, as they had the privileges of the best schools in the country: and the pains taken in their culture at the family fireside insured their improvement in morals.

After preparing himself for college, Mr. Frost's health failed, and his physician advised absolute rest, and insisted that his studies must be pursued privately. He, however, made companions of his books, adding four years of professional study, after which he entered the Methodist ministry. His appointments included some of the best Churches in New England, among them Malden, Charleston, Watertown and Boston. While stationed at Watertown he was married to the youngest daughter of Rev. Geo. Pickering, at that date one of the most noted divines of Methodism. On account of the infirmities of Mrs. Pickering Mrs. Frost soon afterwards was summoned to her father's home to be with and care for her aged parent. This required Mr. Frost to quit the itinerant ranks, but he continued to preach, and at the same time was engaged in teaching as principal of a large and flourishing school.

About the time of the breaking out of the rebellion he was thrown from a carriage receiving such injury as that for four years he did little else than seek restoration. Mr. Frost at this date was living at Cambridge, Massachusetts, and his medical attendants advised a change of climate; and at the same time he received the offer of a situation in 1865 as Purchasing Agent of the Union Pacific railway, requiring his removal to Omaha. He accepted, and, coming west, assumed the duties in connection with the greatest railroad enterprise that had ever before been attempted on the continent. He purchased and shipped materials used in the construction of this overland highway to the amount of $15,000,000, and accounted for it with such precision as to remove all suspicion of dishonesty. He continued in the employ of the corporation till the completion of the road, and afterwards was connected with various enterprises, among which is that of chairman of the building committee of the Omaha High School, a structure costing about a quarter of a million dollars.

Mr. Frost was a member of seven sessions of the legislature of Nebraska. He was appointed agent of the Crow Indians in 1877, and went to the reservation in July of that year on the Yellow-

REV. GEO. W. FROST.

stone river in Montana, where he remained a year and a half. Returning to Omaha he was engaged for some time in settling with the government. There was a disagreement in his and the depart-

ment's accounts, but the matter was adjusted
finally according to his books.

He was a member of the Methodist Ecumenical Council, by the appointment of the American
bishops, which was held in London, England,
September, 1881.

As a writer Mr. Frost's ability was long since
admitted. His numerous contributions both to
the secular and religious press attest the forceful-
ness of his pen.

Mr. Frost was often in the pulpit, and was
regarded an able and instructve preacher of the
gospel; and if his entire time had been given to
the ministry he doubtless would have acquired a
good measure of eminence.

In personal appearance, Mr. Frost was conspicuous. His frame was stalwart, his facial
features indicative of intelligence, and his bearing
that of a refined gentleman. In private he was
sociable and entertaining, and he took pleasure in
making calls on his friends. But he esteemed it a
privilege to mingle in public with his brethren in
using the means of grace. Even when worshiping in the pew the house of God was to him a
favorite resort.

But the time came when he must yield to the
fell destroyer, and his "well-wrought" frame was
prostrated by sickness. He patiently awaited the
summons to leave all pertaining to earth. During
his latest illness and only a few days before his

departure he called his wife and daughter one morning to tell them of the great blessing he received during the night in answer to fervent prayer. Said he, "My whole soul was filled with such joy, rest and peace as I never before experienced." The night before he expired he conceived himself in a great revival. He said to his family, "There are eight hundred conversions! Shout! Shout!" A short time after he said, "Sing, sing;" and himself tried to sing

"Jesus, lover of my soul!"

But his voice faltered before finishing the first line. Again he said, "Sing!" and the hymn was sung through for him. Then he at once sank into unconsciousness, and early on the morning of February 2d, 1888, his spirit passed away in the presence of his family, at his home in Omaha.

CHAPTER XXIII.

METHODISM can hardly do without such men as John Dale. He is a worthy specimen of genial manhood; affable, generous and upright, loving his Church, his family and his home. His social qualities are of an order beyond common, yet he enjoys domestic life and at the same time takes pleasure in the society of his friends, of whom he has many. His business requires close and careful attention, but his office is closed on Sunday.

He is sentimentally a prohibitionist, and advocates the cause believing that the traffic in intoxicants is the worst foe to public morality and good municipal government with which the Churches have to contend. A few years since, in 1888, he was nominated by a State convention as a candidate for Governor on the prohibition ticket.

Mr. Dale has not sought to outgrow the local ministry, though he is in good repute as a preacher, and is often invited to supply pulpits in the vicinity of his home. He is largely interested in building up the Society in his own neighborhood; and has been one of the most enthusiastic instruments and contributors in the erection of the costly and permanent sanctuary in the community where he lives. Except when called upon to officiate else-

where, he is usually engaged on the Sabbath
actively taking part in class, Sunday-school and
Epworth League meetings.

Mr. Dale was honored with an election as delegate to the last General conference by the Lay

REV. JOHN DALE.

Electoral Conference which met in Omaha, September, 1891.

He has pronounced opinions upon most of the
questions now being discussed by the Church at

large, especially such respecting which modifications and other changes are submitted. He belongs neither to the old school nor the new, and is not an extremist in advocating either the needlessness of any change in Church polity or disciplinary law, or, that frequent and radical changes shall be foisted upon the connection by restless and ambitious partisans.

Mr. Dale was born in Yorkshire, England, October 31st, 1832. When the son was two years old his father emigrated to America and settled in Toronto, Canada, where, not long after, his wife died. The son went to an uncle's in the country, remaining till he was sixteen; and in the meantime was converted in a Methodist chapel at the age of twelve years, and began a religious life. The parent had moved to Buffalo, New York, and requested that his son should again be sheltered under the paternal roof, in which city the youth mostly received his education.

Mr. Dale was licensed as a local preacher at Kankakee, Illinois, in 1865; and ordained a local Deacon, at Sterling, in the same State, October 11th, 1874. He came with his family from Kankakee to Omaha in 1885, where he continues to make his home.

CHAPTER XXIV.

BEGINNING in a revival, Methodism has been abundantly sustained by a devoted local ministry. This strong arm of the denomination has been a dependence in saving sinners ever since Mr. Wesley sanctioned, at the instance of his mother, lay preaching. The wisdom of introducing and encouraging the same element in America has been often demonstrated as a fruitful source of awakenings and revivals. Every state in the Union has shared in a religious reformation having been brought about by the preaching of an earnest, self sacrificing local ministry.

Belonging to this same craft is the noisy Scot, Robert Laing, than whom no man is better known in a radius of one hundred miles of Omaha. For many years his labors on both sides of the Missouri have been mostly evangelistic, and in either winter or summer he is ready to engage in revival work. His preaching, praying and singing are fervent and inspiring; and in the great day of reckoning the seals to his ministry will be numerous. He seeks and prefers such a crowning rather than to be esteemed by men either great or learned.

Robert Laing was born in Roxburyshire, Scotland, February 22d, 1830. Leaving his native

country in 1848, he crossed the Atlantic and settled
in Canada, where he lived till he was twenty-four
years old.   He was converted at a Methodist meeting at Gomorrah, Canada, in 1851, and a year later
was licensed to preach.   Soon after receiving

REV. ROBERT LAING.

license he was employed to take charge of a circuit
in the Dominion.   In 1854 he passed the boundary
and landed in the United States, settling temporarily at Council Bluffs, Iowa, where he married

the lady who still shares the pleasure of being his wife.

Soon after arriving at Council Bluffs he was recommended to, and admitted on trial in, the Iowa Annual conference, and was appointed in 1855 to a field of labor including almost all the country between the Missouri river and the Coon fifty or more miles east, and from the Bluffs nearly to Sioux City. The cabins on this circuit were far between in that day, and the settlements few and sparse. Over parts of the territory there were no roads, and nowhere any bridges across the streams. He had to ford the Boyer and Little and Big Sioux rivers in traversing his work; and, besides, endure the cold of winter on long rides over trackless prairies sometimes without seeing a house or fire for twelve hours.

The great area of his circuit and the many discomforts incident to pioneer life were so fatiguing that he closed his engagement at the year's end. In the meantime he decided to try frontier life in another way. White men had begun crossing the river and claiming land in Nebraska. He followed, and made claim to a parcel of prairie in Sarpy county, near Fairview, before the Government surveys were made. On this land he made his home for eighteen years. For the last twenty years his residence has been in Omaha.

Many of the protracted meetings he conducted were continued from two to four weeks, each, and it has been estimated that an average of fifty had been converted each seven days. He claims not that such results were reached by his might or power, but by the spirit of God. He ascribes as a great means of success his method of Bible reading. One interested person said to him, "Brother Laing, I wish you would bequeath to me that Bible of yours: I never heard such a Bible read before." He insists upon the reading of the word of God attentively, studiously, that there may be cultivated in the heart a deepening desire for a closer walk with God.

He was once written to from a distance requesting his assistance at a meeting. He had no money to pay railway fare. The request was so urgent that he was in a quandary as to what he should do. Asking God for help, in an hour money enough came, and he made haste to reach the place from which the request came.

www.ingramcontent.com/pod-product-compliance
Lightning Source LLC
Chambersburg PA
CBHW020513270326
41926CB00008B/857